WITHDRAWN

A Century of Women at Wimbledon

LADIES
OF THE
COURT

VIRGINIA WADE
With Jean Rafferty

New York   ATHENEUM   *1984*

First American Edition

Copyright © 1984 Jean Rafferty

I S B N 0-689-11468-0

Library of Congress Catalog Card Number 83-46158

Printed and bound in Great Britain by
Butler & Tanner Ltd, Frome and London

Wade, Virginia, *1945–*
    Ladies of the court.
    1. Lawn Tennis Championships – History
    2. Tennis players – Portraits   3. Women
    tennis players – Portraits
    I. Title   II. Rafferty, Jean
    796.342′092′2   GV999

    ISBN 0-907516-45-9

Contents

Introduction Page 7

CHAPTER 1 *Beginnings* Page 11

CHAPTER 2 *The Prototype Professional* Page 25

CHAPTER 3 *Theatre on the Centre Court* Page 35

CHAPTER 4 *A Passion for Perfection* Page 51

CHAPTER 5 *Not a Killer at All* Page 67

CHAPTER 6 *The New Wave* Page 77

CHAPTER 7 *The Woman Warrior* Page 87

CHAPTER 8 *The Reluctant Ambassador* Page 97

CHAPTER 9 *The Ultimate Centre Court Player* Page 105

CHAPTER 10 *Grand Slam Greatness* Page 113

CHAPTER 11 *Going for the Big One* Page 121

CHAPTER 12 *Great Expectations* Page 135

CHAPTER 13 *Walkabout at Wimbledon* Page 149

CHAPTER 14 *The First Teenage Prodigy* Page 157

CHAPTER 15 *Staking a Claim to Greatness* Page 171

The Championship Roll Page 183

Biographical Records Page 185

Index Page 190

Introduction

Wimbledon is the Mecca of the tennis world and for one hundred years women tennis players have been making their annual pilgrimage there. It was in 1884 that the first thirteen ladies took to the courts in their long white dresses to play for the All England Club trophy. Like a marriage that improves with time despite the inevitable ups and downs, so Wimbledon and the ladies have grown together. Their mutual respect and esteem have continued to give both the championships and the champions the highest honours. The tournament at Wimbledon is unquestionably the hardest test of all for the players. There is never any speculation about who will enter. Always, every top player is there competing for the title that means the most in tennis.

What a perfect milestone of time one hundred years is to reminisce about those great occasions and personalities that have made history! In twenty-two of those years I've been privileged enough to be included as a participant and oppose the finest exponents of the game in the modern era.

The women's game has always had great appeal, especially on the fast grass of the All England Lawn Tennis Club. It seems that it is easier to identify with than the men's game of superior strength. The women have to develop their attack from a more tactical and strategic approach as they do not have the physical strength simply to overpower an opponent. Nor can any technical flaw be concealed by brute muscular force. As on slower courts where the pace of the men's game is brought to its optimum level, so does the speed of grass compliment the ladies.

In fact the major catalyst in Wimbledon's move from the original Worple Road site to its present Church Road situation in 1922 was a woman. That woman commanded so much attention that a stadium twice its prior size was needed to accommodate the idolising masses. She was, of course, Suzanne Lenglen.

Suzanne was not the first famous lady champion. Maud Watson, Lottie Dod and Dorothea Lambert Chambers were just three of the many famed winners who had illuminated the courts with their varied skills. Without doubt they had those qualities of talent, mental tenacity and physical athleticism that have always been necessary for achieving success. They were distinguished queens of the court, but Suzanne was the first goddess. Her gifts were supreme. Her biting accuracy, coupled with a divine balletic grace, dominated the game for so long without real challenge, that her immortality is unquestioned. Whenever I've spoken to anyone who was fortunate enough to remember her, their eyes light up and they remember her with enormous clarity and veneration. It is one of my great regrets that there are no television tapes of her matches, so that at least we could appreciate her on film.

Even goddesses cannot reign forever, and immediately another dominating champion took over, in the shape of the widely acclaimed beauty, Helen Wills. Here was a winner with totally different attitudes. Her power of concentration was her main weapon, along with infallible groundstrokes. She was an expert surgeon rather than a master painter.

When I look down that long roll of champions, which looks like an imperial family tree, I am reminded how versatile tennis is. Not only are there infinite ways of picking up a tennis racquet and striking a ball, but there is a whole spectrum of personalities who may wield it. The lines that link the family here are only those of common rules, materials and purpose. The rest of the game becomes a kaleidoscope of differing styles and characteristics of personality.

The style of play definitely falls into predominant patterns. A wave of precision groundstroke players becomes replaced by an era of aggressive net-rushers. The American contingent which dominated international tennis immediately before and after the war, did so from the net. From Alice Marble to Doris Hart, they served and volleyed, and came in to the net whenever possible. Then Maureen Connolly swung the pendulum the other way. She won from the back of the court. So too today is Chris Evert's generation of baseliners being gradually replaced by Martina Navratilova's influence.

Over this panoramic span of a century we can track the development of the game, and compare those constant essentials that are required to be a champion. We can also find the factors that vary and change according to the individual or current social trends. The most obvious have been the clothes styles and equipment. It is inconceivable to us now to imagine playing a match in long-sleeved, long-skirted dresses, which would inhibit practically all movement and be horribly constricting – let alone playing with racquets which must have seemed like clubs. Racquets have become progressively lighter. The first racquet I played with, which had endured from the forties, probably weighed sixteen ounces. Now, today's larger racquets are made from composite *metals* and weigh only about twelve ounces. They add power and flexibility to stroke-making. We also play with balls which are tested so rigorously that their bounce is totally consistent. The first balls were covered in flannel and could not have been uniform in reaction for many years.

But the major change in the game has occurred only in the last sixteen years, after tennis became open to professional players in 1968. From that moment tennis has blossomed and expanded from an already large international circuit into a solidly packed twelve-month affair. There are no seasons and off-seasons, no long boat trips searching the sun for outdoor play. One certainly need never become out of practice for match play. In fact, there are probably too many events to follow with any order, and hand in hand with this expansion have come the multiplied pressures. Today's players have even more attention lavished on them, counter-balanced of course by the ensuing demands.

Nevertheless human nature hasn't changed. All the champions began with the same initial stimulus. They had a talent for hitting a tennis ball, they loved exercise, they were mentally fascinated with competition and the challenge of overcoming an opponent. Obviously, they also had an element of showmanship. Originally, if these ingredients existed and nature had thrown them together, you naturally and spontaneously became a fine player. Now, with scientific knowledge you can isolate and develop each of those assets to its highest degree. If a potential champion has a weakness, either technically or mentally, you can train that component separately. The possibility now exists to 'manufacture' players. You can find the technical style which eliminates risk and together with that you can rigorously train the psychological attitudes. At the same time you push the body physically through severe drills and regimen so that it is supremely fit. These methods might produce the majority of players as clones, but in the case of inordinately talented players like Martina Navratilova, it allows the inspiration and spontaneity to reveal itself on a higher level.

The forerunners of our present day heroes (Margaret Court, Billie Jean King, Chris Evert, and Martina Navratilova) reached their successes through their superiority, dedication and ambition.

But the ultimate goal of co-ordination of body and mind was reached through a more naïve approach. As the years have gone by, so has the well of experience deepened, and given the modern champions inspiration and knowledge to learn from.

But whatever the route to that ultimate destination, the thrill of holding that huge silver-gilt salver aloft is the same extraordinary and unforgettable consummation for all the winners.

Simultaneously Wimbledon has grown in the way of a benign patriarch. It is aware of young lifestyles and is part of modern life, but at the same time retains enough tradition to restore the familiarity of perpetual principles. It is vibrantly alive because it keeps abreast of the tennis, but in addition it has that incalculable advantage of its own unique atmosphere that emanates from every blade of grass.

In presenting this book I have depended on the considerable resources and energy of the writer, Jean Rafferty, and the views and content expressed reflect our shared thoughts and opinions. In a few places I have felt it useful to include personal reminiscences, and in this case the change is clearly indicated by the use of italic type. Of course in the chapter which describes my own Wimbledon win, I have depended completely upon the writer, and the views expressed are entirely her own.

No.		Winners of the First Round.	Winners of the Second Round.	Winners of the Third Round.	Winner of the First Prize.
1.	Miss M. Watson	Miss M. Watson	Miss M. Watson	Miss M. Watson	Miss M. Watson
2.	Mrs. A. Tyrwhitt-Drake				
3.	Mrs. C. Wallis	Miss Williams			
4.	Miss B. E. Williams				
5.	Mrs. C. J. Cole	Miss Bingley	Miss Bingley		
6.	Miss Bingley				
7.	Miss F. M. Winckworth	Miss Winckworth			
8.	Miss E. Bushell				
9.	Mrs. G. J. Cooper, w.o.	Mrs. Cooper	Miss Leslie	Miss Watson	
10.	Miss C. Bushell (abs.)				
11.	Miss M. Leslie	Miss Leslie (a bye)			
12.	Miss B. Wallis		Miss Watson		
13.	Miss Watson (a bye)	Miss Watson			

The programme for the very first Ladies Championship at Wimbledon in 1884.

I

Beginnings

IN THE WINTER, without its championship crowds, Wimbledon always seems intensely quiet. The courts, with no lines drawn on them, seem merely strips of grass, as colourless as a bowling green in a municipal park. The stairways without people are cold and vast. There is a feeling of something missing. But in the members' lounge there is a sense of tranquillity, of rightness. It is a serene room, with carefully polished surfaces; a room where tradition is given due respect.

It was Christmas but I would have only two days with my family. I had just flown in from New York but I had a round of business and committee meetings in London before I could get home to Kent for my two days. I would be back in New York on Boxing Day and then it would be Florida, and then talks about a possible documentary

Above: **Sisters Maud and Lilian Watson in the first ever ladies' final at Wimbledon in 1884. Maud beat her elder sister in three sets.**

Opposite: **Lilian Watson** (*top left*) **was the only one of this quartet not to win at Wimbledon. Ernest Renshaw, Lilian, Herbert Lawford and Maud Watson at the Irish Championships in 1884.**

Overleaf: **Tennis was often taken more seriously as a social event than as sport.**

and then . . . Sitting in that lounge at Wimbledon, looking through my mail, my hectic life on the tennis circuit suddenly seemed very far away from the peace there.

Modern tennis has moved on so much from its beginnings. What could there possibly be in common between a player in 1984, the age of jet travel and computers, high speed trains and high speed brains, and a player of 1884, when Queen Victoria was on the throne and life could still be regarded as a fairly manageable enterprise? Could a modern player, with her superior physical fitness and aggressively competitive attitudes, identify with the very first women tennis players?

The letter to *The Times* on June 23, 1884 was emphatic in its reaction to the prospect of women's suffrage. E. Beasley, presumably Mr, of Woodberry Down, thought, 'Its one chance of success, indeed, was that it should be supposed to have no chance of success.' It was a 'tricky and fatal policy', and he looked to all sincere and honourable Conservatives for help in resisting it, he said. (Some would say they are still doing so, a hundred years later.)

It must be supposed that poor E. Beasley had a hard time of it in ensuing years. Women were popping up all over the place. They were in the trade unions, at the universities. And now, that very year, they were even at Wimbledon, thirteen of them, playing for the handsome prize of a silver flower basket valued at twenty guineas. Miss Maud Watson, the winner of that very first ladies' title, did rather well in comparison to some of the champions who followed her. As late as 1960 the winner, Maria Bueno, took away a voucher for only £15.

Tennis was just ten years old when the All England Croquet and Lawn Tennis Club opened the doors of its Worple Road ground to women. Major Walter Clapton Wingfield had applied for a patent for his game, then named 'Sphairistike', only in 1874. But it had instantly proved an ideal game for competition. The men's championship started at Wimbledon in 1877 and only two or three years later the women had a circuit of sorts. The Irish Championships admitted them in 1879 and were followed by tournaments at Bath, Cheltenham, Edgbaston and Exmouth. These tournaments were not restricted to local people and the same players travelled round taking part in them all, not admittedly a very gruelling or lucrative schedule compared to that of the modern women but a true competitive test nonetheless.

The women formed a comparatively small group but there was public interest in them from the first and those who did compete were extremely enthusiastic. One writer, talking of Maud Watson's first ever defeat, compared her to William Renshaw, the great men's champion of the early years, saying that 'had he played in as many open singles during the last three or four years as the lady champion has, we should have expected even his wonderful prowess to have failed him on more than one occasion'.

Interestingly enough, when she first won Wimbledon, Maud Watson already had an unbeaten record going back over three years. In the end her winning streak ran to fifty-five matches, including two Wimbledon titles - only one short of

LAWN TENNIS COSTUMES.

Chris Evert's record on the women's tour almost a century later. But where Chris's streak ran over part of a year, Maud took five years to complete hers, five years of being 'championess', as it was termed then.

Tennis was a social game then for most women, played in long dresses, picture hats, veils and high heels, and even corsets, which were not to disappear till the advent of Suzanne Lenglen, and which were often blood-stained after use, according to the great doubles player of Suzanne's era, Elizabeth Ryan. Maud Watson and her sister Lilian revolutionised tennis dress by wearing separates, silk jersey blouses with long sleeves and low necks, and white wool skirts with a bustle. These were considered rather daring as they came down only to the ankle. Maud also substituted a straw boater like the men's for the picture hat, though she admitted that her hat always flew off in about the third game anyway.

She was talking to the outstanding player of the thirties, Helen Wills Moody. They both stayed at the same country hotel one Wimbledon and compared notes on the game as it was in their respective periods. 'There's certainly more variety in the modern women players' game. And they use their heads more,' Maud told the great American champion.

The one thing that has never varied in the sport, though, is its tension, the pressure it inflicts on the champions. Even in as small a world as that of women's tennis in the 1880s, the pressure of five years of invincibility took its toll on Maud Watson. At the Bath tournament of 1886 it was noted that she had had 'some very hard fights this week, and her nerves are somewhat unstrung'. She was defeated for the first time in her career and the handsome diamond pendant that was the first

prize went to another player.

That player, Lottie Dod, was the first of the teenage prodigies, the first woman to dominate at Wimbledon over a long period, the first real athlete of the game. Even at the age of eleven Lottie had begun to show promise, fulfilled when she won Wimbledon at only fifteen years and nine months, the youngest winner in the hundred years of the Championship.

It might well be said that she was playing a small field, against poor competition, and at a time when the game had hardly developed, and all

Opposite: **Beneath the frills and furbelows the women wore petticoats, corsets, and even bustles.**

Below: **Lottie Dod was still only eleven when she won her first major title, the ladies doubles at the 1882 Northern Tournament at Manchester with her elder sister, Ann, who was nineteen.**

that might be true. But could it have been true of all the sports in which Lottie excelled? She was a remarkable athlete with an exceptional love of competition, an addict, hooked on the excitement of battling against another person. Once she had exhausted the challenge of one sport she simply moved on to another. She won the Ladies' Open Golf Championship at Troon in 1904, played hockey for England, was an expert

Left: **Lottie Dod and Ernest Renshaw at Exmouth in 1888, whether before or after their exhibition match against each other is not certain.** *Above:* **Lottie at the age of fifteen.** *Opposite:* **Punch's view of the 1887 Wimbledon contest.**

skater who passed the tests for both men and women at St Moritz, and an excellent archer, winning an Olympic silver medal in 1908. This fearless sportswoman even added the Cresta Run to her conquests. Five times she was the Wimbledon champion from 1887 to 1893, winning every time she entered though she didn't always bother – one year she went yachting with her sister Ann off the west coast of Scotland instead.

Her final round opponent in most of those years was Blanche Bingley, later Mrs Hillyard. Blanche was one of the most enthusiastic players ever, though not – according to her husband – the most skilful, as she had a 'weakish backhand and total lack of volleying power'. She made up for her deficiencies in technique with her speed around the court, one of the best forehands in the game, and a determined match tempera-

Miss Dod's Service No. 2

ment. 'She never knew when she was beaten or what it was to be tired.'

Commander George Hillyard, though, thought her greatest asset was that thumping great forehand, a completely natural stroke that she couldn't force, but which would just materialise, usually after the season had got under way. Now she would probably have teams of sports scientists examining the fractional movements of the stroke through a computerised camera, as Britain's Jo Durie has done with her serve. Then she just had to wait. Her husband commented, 'Exactly in the same way as there have been great bowlers at cricket who had something peculiar in their action, or the manipulation of their fingers, or both, which caused the ball to "fizz" off the pitch like lightning, so it was with Mrs Hillyard in her drive.'

The lady with the fizz in her fingers was one of a number of people whose lives revolved around tennis. Her husband was secretary of the All

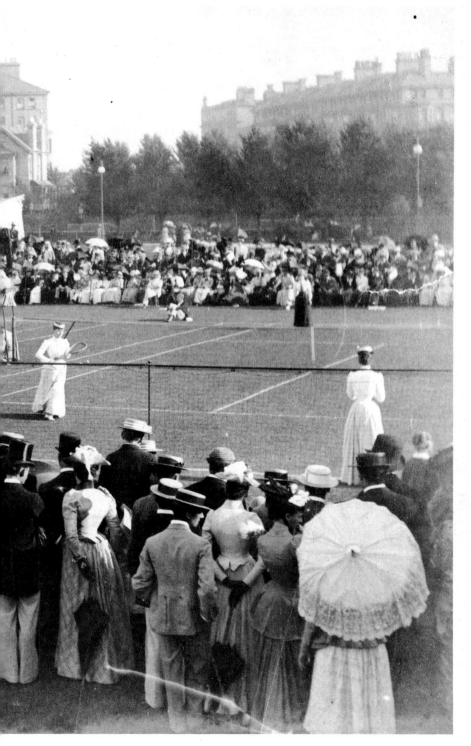

Wimbledon's original site at Worple Road, seen here in the 1890s, is now a girls' school.

England Club right up till 1924 and she herself was one of a group who, he said, 'were keen on the game, and derived so much pleasure from it, that they far preferred to continue playing in public for years after their best had deserted them, rather than allow any consideration for reputation to interfere with their favourite pastime.'

I continue to play selected tournaments, often beating players far ahead of me on the computer rankings but always now playing for pure enjoyment. I think as long as I don't make a fool of myself out there and as long as people are still pleased to see me, and I don't grumble and grouse, then that's fine. I think I accomplish that, and people enjoy watching me play more now because I am more relaxed.

Mrs Hillyard does not appear to have relaxed at all. Throughout the Naughty Nineties while more frivolous spirits were enjoying the delights of the car and the can-can, Mrs Hillyard was amassing a unique Wimbledon record. From 1885, her first final against Maud Watson, to 1901 she was in the final every time she played, no fewer than thirteen times out of seventeen championships. In her first year, 1884, it was the eventual champion who beat her in the second round. Even after this remarkable sequence she continued playing and actually reached the semi-finals in 1912, at the age of forty-eight.

She won Wimbledon six times, a greater number than any other woman of the period, though Lottie Dod was not far behind with five and could presumably have passed that total had she played beyond the age

Blanche Bingley (*below*) **was a six-time winner of Wimbledon. She 'owed as much of her successes to her unconquerable resolution as to her actual strokes', said referee F.R. Burrow. Muriel Robb** (*opposite*) **won the title in 1902. 'The power she got on the ball was astonishing,' said Mrs Hillyard. 'Indeed few men have ever had a harder drive. Fortunately for her opponents she was a player who very decidedly had her days.'**

of twenty-one. Despite Blanche Hillyard's tireless energy and love for the game she never succeeded in beating Lottie at Wimbledon though she had once beaten her when Lottie was just fifteen, Blanche eight years older.

Lottie was the first player in the women's game to approach the fitness and athleticism of the men. When she had first arrived on the tennis scene as a schoolgirl – 'so strong and sturdy' and looking 'so jolly', according to one observer – Lottie had had the advantage of being allowed by convention to play in a shorter skirt than the older women, an advantage she exploited to the full with her exuberant running and jumping. But her real advantage lay in her natural physical strength, speed and co-ordination. Lottie Dod's natural gifts and fierce competitiveness took her closer to the standard of the men of her era than any woman has ever been, before or since. In 1888, then Wimbledon champion, she played the current men's champion, Ernest Renshaw, in an exhibition match and took him to three hard fought sets. The match was, like a great deal of tennis of the day, a handicap one, with Renshaw giving Lottie thirty in every game, but it was still an extraordinary feat and clearly no fluke.

Later that year she actually beat William Renshaw – six times Wimbledon champion and destined to win the following year too – with the same odds.

Although in the fashion of the day, Lottie served underarm and saw no advantage for a woman in attempting to do otherwise, she made no other concessions to feminity. Her great shot was the forehand drive, hit, it was said, with the pace of a man's. 'She uses her shoulders with a freedom we have not noticed in any other lady,' said one writer. But she also had a fine overhead, a backhand that matured over the years from her weakest shot to a very fine and graceful stroke, and a magnificent volley. 'Miss Dod plays doubles as well as most gentlemen, standing on the service line and volleying throughout,' it was said of her.

She made women's tennis into a real sport, disproving those who, in the early years, thought the game was beyond women. She herself was scornful of such an idea. 'There were piteous moans about the weight of the balls, and appeals not to spoil it as croquet had been spoilt, by making it too scientific. It was represented, not it may be hoped by ladies, but on their behalf, that no lady would understand tennis scor-

ing,' she wrote sarcastically.

But it is obvious that all too many women made their femininity an excuse for not trying at sport. Lottie tried in everything and exhorted other women to do the same. 'Ladies should learn to run and run their hardest too, not merely stride,' she said. 'They would find (if they tried) that many a ball, seemingly out of reach, could be returned with ease; but instead of running hard they go a few steps and exclaim, "Oh, I can't" and stop.'

Lottie Dod never indulged in such feebleness, either physically – ease and speed of movement were crucial to her game – or, indeed mentally. George Hillyard thought there was far too much rubbish talked about temperament in those days, but even he conceded Lottie's temperament was admirable for tennis. Her jet black hair and strongly boned face gave her the look of a Red Indian at times, and she seems to have possessed some of that race's impassivity, successfully concealing her emotions in tight situations. *The Pittsburgh Dispatch* said that at 'the tough moments she was a reckless player making many difficult plays with the odds greatly against her where another would hesitate', a comment that was considered a most ridiculous libel by the British newspaper which quoted it. Today we would recognise it for the compliment it is.

Lottie was not reckless, any more than Borg or King or Goolagong were reckless. She merely had the champion's ability to play the most exciting, inventive, daring of shots at her moments of greatest risk. And what modern player would not trade in her topspin double-backhand for a little of that quality?

2

The Prototype Professional

THE FACE WAS GAUNT, long and lean with dark dogged eyes, the chin thrust pugnaciously forward. Long arms hung straight down by her sides and her body was presented square to the camera, almost aggressively. Having her picture taken for the 1913 ladies singles championship at Wimbledon, Dorothea Lambert Chambers stared straight into the camera as if trying to impose her will on the mechanical eye recording her.

Dour, dogged, determined, Mrs Lambert Chambers was the ideal champion to bring women's tennis into the twentieth century, winning seven titles from 1903 to 1914. She was the first woman to realise that tennis is played as much in the mind as with the body. Her mental concentration was unique in her day. She dominated her era by sheer force of will. While the other women of the time were enthusiastic amateurs, Mrs Lambert Chambers was, in her dedication and her ability to exploit her talents to the utmost, the prototype professional.

In the first decade of the twentieth century tennis was still, in many quarters, a primarily social activity. People actually thought of it as just a game and the concept of sport as a matter of life and death or worse was far into the future. 'Some clubs', noted Mrs Lambert Chambers sternly in her book, *Lawn Tennis for Ladies*, 'still use the game for a

garden-party, where long trailing skirts, sunshades and basket chairs predominate. Perhaps a game or two is played in the cool of the evening. That sort of club should be avoided if you are a keen enthusiastic player.'

Mrs Lambert Chambers was, and urged that other women should be too. The world was moving forward. Skyscrapers were going up in American cities, the first radio message had been transmitted across the Atlantic, the Wright brothers had soared into the sky in a powered aircraft – but in Britain the idea of women competing in sport was regarded as at best a joke and more commonly as unnatural and defeminising.

Mrs Lambert Chambers was undaunted by the disapproval of the other half of the British race and felt that sport for women had led to the disappearance of that vexatious species, 'the hysterical female'. This person, she had it on the authority of a doctor friend, 'would put in an appearance obtrusively at critical moments, and the anticipation of a scene always overshadowed his arrangements. We rarely see that type now. Games have driven her away. The woman of the present generation is calm, collected and free from emotional outbursts and I believe that invigorating outdoor exercise is the chief cause.'

Even among the calm, collected women of her generation though, Mrs Lambert Chambers was exceptional. She didn't just take part in sport – she took it seriously. Not all of them did and she once described taking part in a match where she won point after point by drop shotting her opponent. At the end the lady in question indignantly told her that

Parasols for one of Wimbledon's sunny years. But shadows were shortly to fall over Europe in 1914.

May Sutton won the singles in 1905 and 1907. Her great weapon was her forehand drive. F.R. Burrow said she was 'one more proof of how wise it is for ladies who wish to attain the highest honours, at all events as far as singles are concerned, to make back of the court play their chief objective, rather than pursue that will o' the wisp, the volley, which is not suited to their physical powers, except in one case in a million'.

Below: **Playing in the 1906 doubles with Mrs Hillyard, both at the back of the court.**

she did not admire her length, nor think it 'fair to play sneaks'. Dorothea was unimpressed, particularly when her opponent added, 'Anybody could win if they cared to play like that.'

She was a relentless competitor, a phenomenally accurate and steady baseliner determined to impose her rhythm and will on a match. 'What struck one in particular was the way she manoeuvred for her openings,' commented George Hillyard. 'She always appeared to be thinking several strokes ahead. No player ever used the wits le bon Dieu had given

them to greater purpose.' Norah Gordon Cleather, later assistant secretary at the club, remembered being taken to Wimbledon as a child and even then noticing, 'The curious intensity of purpose that her bent shoulders seemed to impart to her every movement on the court.'

The effect on her opponents must have been crushing. 'Few indeed have been able to induce such a feeling of hopelessness in her opponents as she did,' said F.R. Burrow, the Wimbledon referee. The modern champion who comes closest to Mrs Lambert Chambers' imposing style is Chris Evert-Lloyd, who has a similar effect on those who play her and has similar technique.

When I was playing full-time, she was a master, a real master. She would absolutely pin you. With an attacking player like me, first, her passing shots are so good. Her serve isn't so good but she gets a lot of first serves in and that isn't easy to do.

She has a fantastic mind. If you get involved in anything from the baseline she just pins you deeper and deeper and deeper. She'd hit to my backhand which wasn't my aggressive shot and then she'd be moving in to the court and you'd be moving backwards and working much, much harder than she was. She'd be taking the ball early and you'd be taking it late and then she'd have a set up and that would be it. I usually had the feeling that I was getting pinned on the back fence and she was getting bigger and bigger and bigger.

Mrs Lambert Chambers loomed too, a threateningly large figure above her contemporaries, though it's doubtful whether there were many of the calibre of today's top players. There was Charlotte Cooper who won the title five times from 1895 onwards, including once as late as 1908 when, as Mrs Sterry, she unexpectedly beat Mrs Lambert Chambers in the semis. 'Chattie'

Charlotte Cooper, later Mrs Sterry, won the title five times, in 1895, 1896, 1898, 1901 and 1908. She had 'the quickness of foot and anticipation that enabled her to cover an extraordinary amount of the court', said George Hillyard. *Below:* On her way to the 1908 title against Miss Morton.

Cooper Sterry tumbled through the pages of Wimbledon history with a charming vigour, the possesser of an attractive attacking game, in an age when most women longed wistfully to be able to drive with the power and accuracy of Mrs Lambert Chambers. Mrs Sterry, according to Mr Hillyard, was 'a quite unusually strong and active girl, with a constitution like the proverbial ostrich, who scarcely knew what it was to be tired, and was never sick or sorry. She once told me she had heard of such things, but she did not know what a headache was'. Mrs Lambert Chambers' hysterical female would not have known what to make of her.

But the woman who came closest to challenging Dorothea Lambert Chambers was May Sutton, the first woman from overseas to win the Wimbledon title. The custom then, as indeed for over half the twentieth century, was for visiting players to be offered accommodation in private homes, and Miss Sutton, then only seventeen years old, had the pleasure of staying with Mr and Mrs Hillyard. George Hillyard saw her at dinner on her first night and didn't rate her prospects of being a good tennis player very highly.

'My first impression was of a nice-looking rather short girl, with very broad shoulders, in a pretty muslin dress cut in an old-fashioned style, and altogether, to my way of thinking, too powerfully built for speed about a court. On retiring to our rooms I said to my wife, "There my dear, I told you so, another dark horse, much too heavy for lawn tennis, nothing to fear from her." Well, appearances are proverbially deceptive, as we were to find out the very next day when the young lady in question gave us most convincing proof both of her wonderful play and ability of getting to and returning balls from remote parts of the court by beating my wife and Miss Connie Wilson (another player of the first rank) one after the other.'

She also beat Mrs Lambert Chambers in the Wimbledon final. To succeed at the highest level, then as now, it was necessary to possess one great, crushing morale-boosting weapon, one stroke that can pull a

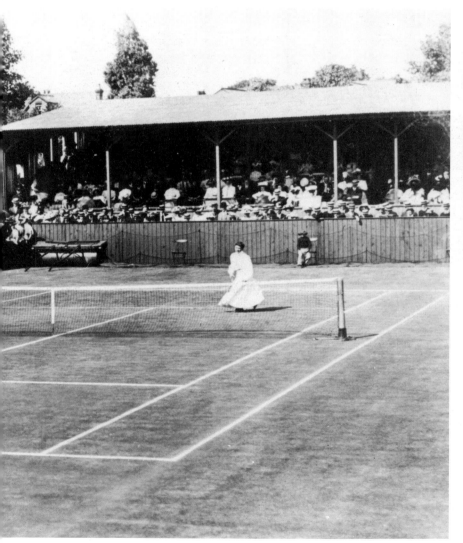

match your way. In May Sutton's case that weapon was a crunching forehand drive that was too much for most of the women of the day to handle. That weapon was functioning perfectly in 1905, though *The Times* observed that Mrs Lambert Chambers was playing with a bandaged wrist and that her only tennis practice that year had been during the Wimbledon fortnight.

She was better prepared in 1906 when she again faced Miss Sutton in the final. There were four thousand people there to watch, a small number in comparison with today's Centre Court capacity of 13,500. But that tough, determined compet-

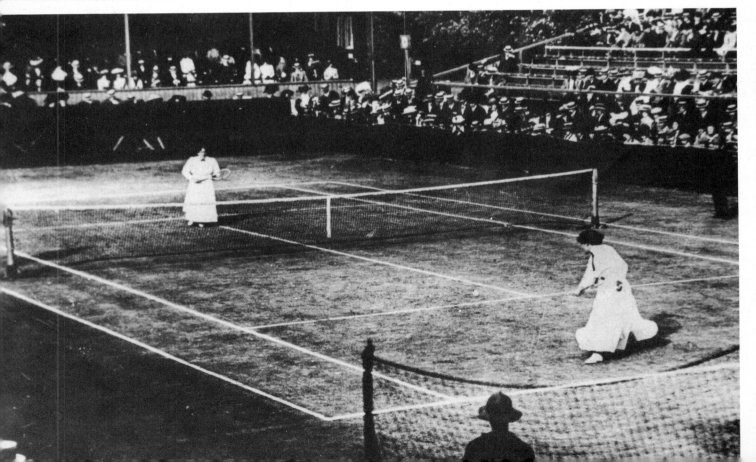

itor, Dorothea Lambert Chambers, confessed to feeling 'helpless and destitute' in front of so many people. Miss Sutton, she deduced, must have felt even lonelier, being so far away from home.

We tend to think of pressure in sport as being the product of our high powered, high tension, high speed modern life. But it's there simply when one person has to win and the other lose, whether thousands of dollars depend on the outcome or not. It's there in Dorothea's own account of the match. 'I have never had such a craving to speak to someone as I had in this match,' she said. 'Just one friendly word to tell me whether I was playing the right sort of game or not. I confess my feelings were very strung up,' so much so that she actually asked the umpire's opinion of her tactics when they changed ends. In true Wimbledon tradition his face remained a mask, though he later told her he had wanted to say, 'I don't know, but stick to it whatever happens.'

She did, eventually managing to block out the shouts of encouragement from the crowd, and the pitched battle in the stands when a lady refused to put her sunshade down. If May Sutton's great weapon was her forehand, Dorothea's was her concentration. 'You *must* lose yourself in the game,' she said. 'Eye, mind, hand all working together. If you find that events transpiring outside the court are attracting your attention you cannot be watching the ball.'

Perhaps because concentration is usually such a hard quality to win, Dorothea Lambert Chambers was late in coming to her full maturity as a player. Her greatest years were between the ages of thirty-one and thirty-five, though she had a been playing tennis all her life, even remembering playing up against a brick wall in her parsonage home as

Opposite, top right: **Mrs Lambert Chambers receiving her Olympic gold medal from Queen Alexandra in 1908, the only time the tennis Olympics were staged at Wimbledon;** *below:* **In action against Miss Boothby in the 1910 final**

a child, 'with numerous dolls and animals of all kinds as spectators – really as big a gate as we get now at some tournaments. Each toy in turn was chosen as my opponent. Needless to say, I always won these matches. My adversaries took very little interest in the proceedings.'

In later life she was to discover that there was still very little interest in the proceedings from others. Women tennis players were second-class citizens, put on poor

courts and given an assortment of huts and outhouses to change in. Only at Wimbledon and Queens did the women's dressing room even have a bathroom. 'I am sure if men had to experience the changing room accommodation afforded for our use there would not be many of them competing at tournaments,' she remarked acidly.

Although she played the traditional women's game, the baseline game, Dorothea was not quite the traditional passive woman. She was never afraid to speak out. It was a time of increasing militance by the suffragettes and even Wimbledon itself was the subject of an attack, unsuccessful in the end as a night watchman had been hired. There was never any suggestion that Dorothea was a feminist, but she did disagree strongly with the prevailing notion of women being frail. 'Is the essential feature of a woman her weakness, just as the essential feature of a man is his strength, not merely physical but mental and moral strength? I do not think so. Woman is a second edition of man, if you will; therefore, like most second editions, an improvement on the first,' she said. She even objected to the unspoken requirement that women should behave in a pretty manner on the court, creating no unseemly impressions of effort or emotion. She wanted women to be natural. 'I prefer that she should show some signs of excitement, that her muscles should be strained and her face set,' she said defiantly. It's hard to imagine her enjoying being part of the Avon circuit of recent years and being told, 'You've never looked so good.'

She won her last title in 1914, on the eve of the Great War, when women's reserves of strength, mental, physical and moral, would be needed as never before.

PHOTOGRAPHS BY SPORT AND GENERAL.

1. MRS. O'NEILL.
2. MRS. PARTON.
3. MRS. HANNAM.

4. MRS. SATTERTHWAITE.
5. MISS TULLOCH.
6. MRS. HILLYARD.

7. MRS. TUCKEY.
8. MRS. STERRY.
9. MRS. EDGINGTON.

10. MISS H. AITCHISON.
11. MRS. LAMBERT CHAMBERS.
12. MRS. LARCOMBE.

13. MISS HOLMAN.
14. MRS. MACNAIR.
15. MISS D. P. BOOTHBY.

Picture spread from the
Illustrated London News **of 1913.**

3

Theatre on the Centre Court

SUZANNE LENGLEN was just a child before the war, a dark perky child with an urchin grin and a squirrel's bright eyes and an irrepressible vitality that gave her a jaunty look even when she was standing still. She was just a child of thirteen when she first played doubles with Elizabeth Ryan; just a child, a head shorter than the adults, when she won the World Hard Court Championship in 1914. Just a child who didn't know then that she'd lost part of her childhood.

The little girl's immediate facility with a tennis raquet at the age of eleven had led her father to start coaching her. He wanted her to beat the world and her natural talent made him think she could. He drove her but she learned quickly because she wanted to learn. The Lenglen family lived in Nice on the French Riviera and many fine tennis players came to winter there. Charles Lenglen admired the play of the cool, indefatigable English women, the length and accuracy of their drives, the quiet logic of the way they placed the ball. But even more he admired the play of the men, their attack, their speed, the way they used the whole court. His daughter would beat all the women because she would learn to play like a man.

Suzanne was not a beautiful woman, but she was a glamorous one and the people who crowded into

Above left: **Ethel Larcombe in action. She won the title in 1912.**
Above: **Suzanne Lenglen, posing for a publicity picture in 1920, the year she won her second Wimbledon final.**

Wimbledon in unprecedented numbers that first year after the war all wanted to see her. The interest was so great that the ladies' matches, which rarely started till mid-way through the tournament, had to begin on the first Tuesday. Suzanne's opponent was so unused to play starting so early that she hadn't even brought her playing costume with her. The crowds were not disappointed. Some were shocked, walking out of her matches when they saw the thin silky dresses which clung to that chic form or when she took out her makeup and re-touched her face between sets. But her tennis was even more extraordinary than they had been led to believe. Mrs Larcombe, the 1912 champion, and a player who was famed for her tactical astuteness, was expected to do well against her but she ran out of tactics. Everything she tried only

succeeded in acting as a foil to Suzanne's gifts. 'The lob – Mrs Larcombe specialises in lobs – was just a windfall to her smash,' said *The Times*. 'The drop then, and make her run! (Mrs Larcombe's drops are things connoisseurs rave about) – but the drop showed that if lawn tennis was this Atalanta's recreation, running is her forte. The drop did make her run – if run is not too strenuous a word for her fluent motion – and there she was, where she wanted to be, at the net.'

But Mrs Larcombe, fine player though she was, did not have that air of invincibility that Mrs Lambert Chambers carried with her on to the Centre Court. The greatest woman player in the world, Dorothea was the epitome of all those cool, indefatigable Englishwomen Charles Lenglen had watched so often on the Riviera. At the time she was forty

years old, twice as old as Suzanne, but so great was her reputation that the question buzzing around London during Wimbledon fortnight was whether Suzanne could beat her, not the other way round.

Their match was one of the greatest, most competitive finals Wimbledon has ever seen, unrivalled for length until Margaret Court and Billie Jean King, the two great champions of the sixties, fought it out for the first title of the next decade. As a great dramatic spectacle it was possibly even more satisfying than the 1970 final, where the two players had a similar game. But in 1919 Mrs Lambert Chambers was the great baseliner, steady, dogged, with supreme mental concentration. Suzanne was as shrewd tactically but her game was more brilliant. Fast, spectacular, fluid, she leapt across the court with the explosive

Above and opposite: **Dorothea Lambert Chambers and Suzanne Lenglen in their epic final of 1914. Suzanne's dramatic personality and showmanship were new in tennis. So were her clothes. She liberated women tennis players from the long skirts and layers of petticoats they had worn up until then, though her shorter skirts and figure-hugging dresses shocked some spectators.**

grace of a cat, like a cat landing softly before you had worked out where the movement started. The winners seemed to come from nowhere. The word 'genius', with its suggestion of inspirational play, is used so often about her that it's probable her greatness, like that of Maria Bueno and Evonne Goolagong many years later, lay in this quality of unexpectedness. Unlike them her unpredictability was coupled with clear think-

ing, exceptional accuracy and rock solid stroke production. She really was the complete player.

She was not as experienced as Mrs Lambert Chambers though, and that first final went to a set each. In the interval Suzanne had her customary brandy, but her opponent had nothing. 'I felt cold in the third set and could have done with a stimulant myself,' she said, 'except that such a thing was not English.' But her stiff upper lip failed her in the final set when at 6–5 she had two match points and failed to clinch them. 'I lost my concentration in thoughts of how the newspapers, which had strongly backed Suzanne, would have to climb down,' she said ruefully afterwards.

Suzanne's win deprived Mrs Lambert Chambers of a record eighth title, but for Suzanne it had even more far-reaching consequences. Dorothea Lambert Chambers believed it gave her an obsessional need to win, that her desire for victory sprang not from competitiveness but from a deep neurotic compulsion. This may well have been true, for Suzanne displayed no real pleasure in competition. The wide smile, so spontaneous when she was a child, became strained and artificial. Many things about her were artificial – her grand entrances, her retinue of admirers, the way she posed like a fashion model, hand on hip and coat thrown back, whenever she went on court.

And at times her behaviour was so extreme, her distaste for the pressures of competition so intense, that Mrs Lambert Chambers must have thought her old friend the hysterical female was a model of restraint. Not until John McEnroe came along sixty years later did anybody show so clearly the intolerable strain that could be placed on a player by the sport.

The cracks first began to show clearly in 1921, when against her father's advice Suzanne agreed to tour America in aid of the war-damaged French villages. The long crossing in a liner aggravated her chronic asthma so badly that she declared herself unfit to play in the American championships the following day. Suzanne was persuaded to change her mind, her first round opponent was persuaded to scratch; but her second round opponent was

Elizabeth Ryan won nineteen doubles titles at Wimbledon, six of them with Suzanne. One observer, seeing them both together, thought Elizabeth seemed like an amazon, 'whose heaviness and masculine efficiency on the court were the very antithesis of Suzanne's dancing grace'.

Opposite: 'As an illustration of her lissomness, I once saw her, in a match, suspect something wrong with the sole of one of her shoes. Instead of picking her foot up in front of her to look at the sole, she flung it up *backwards* on her shoulder and just turned her head to have a good look at it *there* – all this on the court, without support of any kind.' – Mrs Larcombe on Suzanne.

Molla Mallory the defending champion, and she couldn't be persuaded to do anything other than go all out to beat Suzanne. An aggressive, hard-hitting baseliner, Molla won the first set 6–2 and was leading 2–0 in the second – it was all too much for a debilitated Lenglen, who fled the court in tears, leaving pandemonium behind her.

That she genuinely had been ill was beyond question, though there were other instances where the illnesses appeared to be inside her head. Earlier that year, after a hard match against Kitty McKane (later Mrs Godfree), she had wanted to default from the final of a tournament in Brussels. But no doctor would sign her unfit and she was obliged to play, easily winning against her friend Elizabeth Ryan. The fact was that she was a class above the other competitors of her day, fine players though they were, but it took such great efforts of will-power for her to hone her nerves to the correct pitch that sometimes she didn't have any energy left over for playing. Often she was found retching in the dressing room before a match and her hysterical tantrums off court could be as spectacular as her play on.

In fact, wearing though it may have been for those around her, Suzanne had a remarkable big match temperament. Mrs Hazel Wightman remembered seeing her at Wimbledon in 1924 when, still recovering from the effects of jaundice, she was clearly suffering in a match against Elizabeth Ryan, the player famed for the record number of doubles titles she won at Wimbledon. But she was a formidable competitor in singles as well. 'It took grit to keep on with defeat staring her in the face, and she proved herself a good sport,' wrote Mrs Wightman. Kitty Godfree, the attractive attacking player who was to win Wimbledon twice

during those years, was even more emphatic about the notorious Lenglen temperament.

'Many people who are not very well acquainted with the game itself or with her play, are under the impression that the French lady champion has been handicapped throughout her career by a nervous temperament. I consider that almost the opposite is the truth, and that she has had so much success because she is keyed up to the highest pitch all the time. But the ability to be always keyed up obviously imposes

Above: **Suzanne Lenglen with Molla Mallory, the only player ever to defeat her in her senior career, albeit through default at the 1921 US Championships. Their next meeting was eagerly anticipated by the tennis public and came the following year in the 1922 Wimbledon final. Molla's husband bet $10,000 that his wife would win. She didn't. Suzanne took just twenty-seven minutes to beat her, for the loss of only two games.**

Right: **Suzanne with Helen Wills, before the only match they ever played, in Cannes in 1926.**

after her own career was over she played a practice match with Helen Jacobs and the American recalled that though there was an important quarter final match going on in the main stadium at Roland Garros, hundreds of spectators swarmed round to watch them play. At the end of an hour and a half's practice Helen Jacobs was more exhausted than she had ever been after an actual match. 'She was the greatest woman I ever saw,' she says now. 'You couldn't really win points aginst her – she had to make an error. And Suzanne Lenglen rarely, rarely made a mistake.'

She was a heady mixture, a supremely accurate driver of the ball who knew exactly what margin of error to allow herself, yet an artist who could pull off the impossible from any part of the court. She was *the* player for the Jazz age, gay, brittle and brilliant. She had style and such glamour that the white rabbit fur coat she wore was always called ermine in the newspapers. The Lenglen bandeau was copied all over the world and not just for tennis – for cocktails and riding in fast cars and dancing fast dances. With her silky dresses Lenglen showed the world that being shocking didn't have to be anything as serious as an act of defiance – it could be fun. On the Riviera, where she lived, her daily matches were as much a part of the social ritual as mid-morning champagne or the thé dansant at four o'clock or the visit to the casino at night.

But behind the glittering exterior lay hours and years of practice, of pressure from her parents, of a pursuit of perfection that took her beyond the limits of amateurism into the territory of the artist. So intense was that pursuit that she – and her parents – were distraught if she missed a shot. Bill Tilden, her male counterpart, would throw away

the severest strain on the nerves. Her record shows it. No player in the world has played a bigger continuous series of matches in which topmost form has been maintained. All other successful players have had more lapses involving defeat, and no other player has had to sustain the strain of so much public comment and expectation. It may be urged that it is impossible always to be at one's best physically as well as intellectually, but it seems to me that Mlle Lenglen has come nearer to it than any other player.'

She went undefeated in tournament play over seven years, winning six Wimbledon singles titles, six French, the Olympic gold in 1920 and a clutch of doubles titles too. More popular, more publicised even than Big Bill Tilden, the great male player of the era, it was her popularity that finally forced Wimbledon's move from its original site in Worple Road to bigger purpose-built premises in Church Road. After 1919 she rarely had a close match at Wimbledon but people didn't care. They just wanted to see her play. Years

whole sets to show how he could toy with his opponents but Suzanne's showmanship was completely lacking in malice. 'She had a stride a foot and a half longer than any known woman who ever ran,' said Elizabeth Ryan. 'But all those crazy leaps she used to take were done after she hit the ball. Sure, she was a poser, a ham in the theatrical sense. She had been spoiled by tremendous adulation from the time she was a kid, but she was the greatest woman player of them all. Never doubt that.'

The last great match of her career was not at Wimbledon, nor indeed at any major tournament, but it was invested with more publicity and razzamatazz than was probably ever seen for any sporting event till Muhammad Ali had his 'Rumble in the Jungle' with George Foreman in Zaire. The Carlton Club in Cannes was not quite as exotic a location as the stadium in Kinshasa, though Helen Wills, the cool and bemused observer of the whole crazy proceedings as well as one of the two protagonists, had never experienced any-

thing like it before. 'There seemed nothing to do there but seek ways of passing the time pleasurably,' she noted.

At twenty-one she was already a three time winner of the US National Championships and an Olympic gold medallist in both singles

The sunshine and palm trees of the Riviera usually provided a more relaxed setting for Suzanne's tennis than Wimbledon ever could. But her tense match against Helen Wills in Cannes was an exception. *Right:* **She shakes hands with the American, but the match – contrary to appearances – was not over yet.**

and doubles. Her sense of realism told her that much of the fuss was because the sports pages were notoriously slow in February, but she probably underestimated the intense public interest both in Lenglen and in the fact that a challenger had come along who had a real chance of dislodging her from her supremacy. To Helen Wills, the whole thing seemed almost unreal, a dream in which tennis matches, tea dances and smart restaurants passed by to occasional glimpses of Lenglen emerging from cars in her white coat and rose coloured bandeau. 'Mlle Lenglen was always the central figure of a group in which vociferous and intense conversation was being carried on,' she recalled.

One of those vociferous and intense conversations apparently went on the very night before the match. While Helen Wills slept peacefully

THE QUEEN GREETS THE REIGNING "QUEEN" OF THE LAWN-TENNIS COURTS :
HER MAJESTY SHAKING HANDS WITH MLLE. LENGLEN.

On the left, Queen Mary shakes hands with Suzanne Lenglen at the Jubilee Centenary of 1926. Only a few days later Suzanne's bid for her seventh title was to end in chaos.

Below: The Jubilee line-up of champions. The ladies, from the left, are Maud Watson, Blanche Hillyard, Lottie Dod, Charlotte Sterry, Dorothea Lambert Chambers, Dora Boothby, Ethel Larcombe, Suzanne Lenglen and Kitty Godfree.

in her hotel, Mama and Papa Lenglen were said to have been urging Suzanne on, reminding her of the honour that was at stake the next day and saying 'all the things it's unwise to say to even the most phlegmatic player the night before an important match' according to Sarah Palfrey Cooke some years later. Lenglen finally went to bed at two thirty in the morning, some five hours after Helen Wills.

But she took the first set the following day before four thousand people in the ground and countless others outside popping their heads up through the red-tiled roofs of their villas.

There were people clinging to eucalyptus trees watching till the gendarmes drove them out – and took over the trees themselves. Suzanne took frequent sips from her silver brandy flask, particularly in the second set, when at times she looked near collapse. The set swung from one to the other, as first Helen's hard hitting dominated, then Suzanne's artistry.

But the most spectacular moment of all came at 6–5, match point to Suzanne. Helen's forehand whipped across court past the Frenchwoman, only to land so close to the line that at first it was thought out. The match was awarded to Suzanne, the officials began to gather, when suddenly it was announced that Helen's shot had been in after all and the point was hers. Not surprisingly Suzanne lost that game and it wasn't till a full ten minutes later that she finally took the set – and the match.

Suzanne was sobbing, photographers were crowding round,

Suzanne arrives at Wimbledon in 1933, still greeted by big crowds even though she had not played there for seven years.

floral arrangements six feet high were being brought on to the court. Helen Wills just walked quietly away. She was never to play Suzanne Lenglen again.

But she was to encounter her later that year, Wimbledon's Jubilee year, and the year when Lenglen walked away from tournament tennis – though certainly not quietly. Her row with Wimbledon referee F.R. Burrow was a messy affair, with both sides claiming not to have received the communications the other claimed to have sent. Suzanne thought she had one match to play, Burrow had her down for two. The upshot was that Suzanne arrived too late for the first as Queen Mary waited patiently for her to arrive. When she did, Burrow publicly ticked her off. Humiliated and hysterical the champion retreated to her dressing room.

Helen Wills, out of the championship after a bout of appendicitis, was in the audience that day, waiting for the match to begin. When she realised nothing was happening she went round to the dressing rooms. 'From behind the white door of the dressing room which had on it the words in gold lettering "The Lady Champion", one could hear the sound of weeping. So I quickly left, and that is all I know about the incident, except that people usually have a reason when they cry, and the reason must have been a real one, because Wimbledon meant much to Mlle Lenglen.'

It did, very much. When the crowd turned on Suzanne several days later as she came out to play a mixed doubles partnering Jean Borotra it must have seemed as if her

The garden party image of tennis, all
sunshine and straw hats, is beautifully
captured by Sir John Lavery's painting of
1895, *A Rally*. But beneath the pretty
dresses the ladies' restrictive corsets
were often stained with blood.

PLAYER'S

FITZ-GERALD

Tobacco & Cigarettes

PLAYER'S NAVY CUT

ISSUED BY THE IMPERIAL TOBACCO CO. (OF GREAT BRITAIN AND IRELAND), LIMITED.

For freshness, charm & sweet attractiveness Use GOODWIN'S Toilet Soap

Bovril keeps you fit!

Tennis, with its associations of good health, fitness and fun, has been used by advertisers since the 1920s to promote their products – a process that continues today in a somewhat more sophisticated form.

Below: a delicate watercolour of Suzanne Lenglen painted by Helen Wills Moody.
Left: Helen started the fashion for eyeshades but the slinky dress and dramatic pose are pure Lenglen.
Opposite: Suzanne models her latest tennis outfit for the photographers in 1925.

LA VIE PARISIENNE

Samedi 27 Juillet 1929

Que préférez-vous, Messieurs ?
Le bandeau Lenglen ou la visière Wills ?

whole world was turning on her. She and Borotra won their match, but she scratched from all her events and turned professional a short time after.

It seems she was happy in later life. She lived a normal life for the very first time, enjoyed romance, even, finally, toured the States. Alice Marble remembers, as a little girl, seeing her when she came to San Francisco. 'I'm ashamed to say I fell asleep,' she remembers. 'It was ten o'clock at night and the room was smokey. But I remember she just seemed to leap into the ball. She never seemed to be on the ground at any time. She had to be the greatest player ever.'

In later years she set up a coaching school in Paris. She loved teaching children and was happier and more relaxed than she had ever been. She was only thirty-nine when she died of leukemia in 1938. And it is still very hard, even with our super powerful, super efficient modern game to get anyone who ever saw her to admit they've ever seen a better woman tennis player.

Suzanne, despite the sarcasm of this cartoon in the *New Yorker*, had never played tennis just for sport. She had always been compulsive, driven – playing more for the sake of winning than for any pleasure in the game. Ironically, turning professional freed her. 'At last,' she said, 'after fifteen years of torture, I can enjoy my tennis.'

"Pour le Sport"

4

A Passion for Perfection

GEORGE BERNARD SHAW was in his most provocative playful mood. Tennis, he said, with a sly look at the lady champion sitting by the fire, should be played only in the long grass in the meadows – and in the nude. The lady champion tried not to let a flicker of expression cross her face. It can safely be assumed that Helen Wills Moody, popularly known as Miss Poker Face, succeeded.

She was probably the most controlled champion the game has ever seen, a woman whose expression did not change even on the rare occasions when she lost. More remarkable still, it did not change when she won, which was practically all the time. She won a record eight Wimbledon singles titles and in five years from 1927 to 1932 did not lose a set to anyone, much less a match. But her equanimity in the face of victory was unsurpassed, even by those imperturbable stars of the modern era, Bjorn Borg and Chris Evert. They may not have registered distress at defeat, but you could always tell from their expressions that they liked to win. Mrs Moody did not reveal even that much.

Even as a young girl she controlled her emotions to an unhealthy degree. Helen Jacobs, later to become her greatest rival during the thirties, remembered playing a practice game with her when she was eighteen, Jacobs three years younger. 'I had been used to more informality in practice games, and even in matches, than the rather stony solemnity of this presumably casual meeting. At fifteen one is pretty impressionable, and I wondered then if the unchanging expression of my opponent's face and the silence when we passed at the net on odd games, were owing entirely to deep concentration, or whether they weren't perhaps a psychological weapon.'

At the time of this first meeting Helen Wills was already the US champion, a distinction she had achieved at the age of only seventeen. But even this triumph left her unmoved. 'Had anyone told me that I was to be champion of the United States,' she said, 'I would have thought that I would be so full of joy that life itself would be painful to live. And now that I had actually won, things didn't feel different at all. I was delighted and happy of course but the universe had not changed.' Her triumphal celebrations consisted merely of a shockingly unathletic breakfast of rich pastry and hot chocolate with whipped cream.

That first major championship

win had ended on a rather curious note. The umpire, inspired by enthusiasm either for her flawlessly cool tennis or her flawlessly cool beauty, jumped down from his chair and kissed her, an attention she bitterly resented. John Olliff of the *Daily Telegraph* pointed out that, while such an incident could never have happened in England, it would probably have been received with enthusiasm in a Latin country. Helen Will's reaction, he wrote, 'suggests something very cool and calm and almost precious in her character. She proved later to be emotionless without being passionless, a remarkable combination.'

Emotionless, because passion crowded out everything else, left no room for trivial personal feelings. Helen Wills Moody's passion was for perfection, for supreme achievement, for the unreachable. Her outward impassivity concealed a raging restlessness to perform at the highest, and most beautiful level, in everything she did. She was an accomplished artist who had several exhibitions of her work in London and New York, a fine writer, and a diligent student who cried at school when she did not get one hundred per cent for spelling. She said she would have done the same at college if she had not gained the highest honour, a Phi Beta Kappa key, for her scholarship.

On the tennis court her great art was to conceal the fact that she was striving at all. Cold, inhuman, beautiful, she seemed untouched by the nervous stress felt by more vulnerable creatures who lacked her terrifying inner certainty that she would win. She was detached, as if moving in some protective space capsule

AMERICA'S LADY LAWN-TENNIS CHAMPION IN ENGLAND: AT PRACTICE.

PHOTOGRAPHS BY SPORT AND GENERAL, AND L.N.A.

MISS HELEN WILLS PRACTISING AT WIMBLEDON:
THE BEGINNING OF THE BACKHAND DRIVE.

MISS HELEN WILLS SERVING: A PHOTOGRAPH
AT WIMBLEDON.

MISS HELEN WILLS'S BACKHAND DRIVE: THE FINISH
OF THE STROKE.

ANOTHER PHASE OF HER SERVICE: MISS HELEN
WILLS IN PLAY.

HOW THE AMERICAN LADY LAWN-TENNIS CHAMPION GRIPS HER RACKET: MISS HELEN WILLS
GIVES A DEMONSTRATION AT WIMBLEDON.

A NEWCOMER TO WIMBLEDON OF WHOM GREAT
THINGS ARE EXPECTED THIS YEAR.

that sealed her off from the effects of tension or fatigue or pain. But she created that effect only by extreme effort and concentration, as Norah Gordon Cleather, then assistant secretary at Wimbledon, discovered by accident one day. 'I picked up her middy blouse that had fallen on the floor and, to my amazement, I found it was as heavy as lead and soaked with perspiration. I suddenly realised that Helen's apparent impassiveness was a mask. We had seen so much of that mask, it was quite startling to find that underneath it Little Poker Face was human after all.'

The mask was a weapon, as valuable in its way as her formidably powerful groundstrokes, her absolute concentration, the uncanny anticipation that made up for her lack of speed around the court. In a sense too the mask was real. Helen Wills

Left: **Helen on her first trip to Wimbledon in 1924.**
Below: **Helen in the only match she ever lost at Wimbledon, the 1924 final, to Kitty McKane.**

Moody had the rare ability, at moments of crisis, to transform the passion for perfection, her monumental desire for supremacy, into a cold hard composure that she turned on her opponents. 'There is no proof that people do not become more calm at a difficult moment than more nervous,' she said, and was testimony of her own theory whenever she competed.

She expressed overt emotion about a match only a few times in her life, once near the beginning of her international career when she lost the 1924 Wimbledon final to Kitty McKane and cried quietly in the dressing room after, the only time she wept over tennis; once after the thrilling final of 1935 when Helen Jacobs held match point against her, only to lose. Afterwards she flung her arms round Sir Herbert Wilberforce, then Chairman of the All England Club, and kissed him. 'I had always wanted to because he was so sweet,' she said. Then, at the very end of her career, when she reached match point for her eighth title, she gave a warm slow smile, a small thing in others but unique for her.

Her 1924 final against Kitty McKane was the last match she lost at Wimbledon. The Englishwoman won the title again in 1926, the year of the Lenglen debacle, but after that it was virtually the property of Helen Wills any time she came to claim it. In the next twelve years she fought and won eight championships, a greater number of titles than any other player, man or woman. Cilli Aussem, the delightfully doll-like German player whose footwork, though not her sense of adventure, was said to resemble Lenglen's, won in 1931 against her compatriot Hilde Krahwinkel (later Sperling). Then British dreams of glory were satisfied when Dorothy Round, hard hitting off the court and on, won in

1934 and again in 1937. Mrs Moody's other missing year, 1936, was taken by Helen Jacobs, who was runner-up at Wimbledon no less than five times.

Helen Jacobs in fact was Helen Wills Moody's opponent in half her finals, coming closest to beating her in 1935, when she held match point at 5-2 in the third.' She had her stone cold,' remembers Lance Tingay, formerly tennis correspondent of the *Daily Telegraph*. 'Somehow Helen Wills got a return, a silly little poop of a shot, a lob. Helen Jacobs was normally very good at the net but a gust of wind deflected the ball slightly. She was very nervous and she

Lilli de Alvarez lost three finals in a row at Wimbledon, one to Kitty Godfree (left), and two to Helen Wills. But she was one of the most exciting players ever seen there, always trying to win points in the most spectacular way possible.

just put it into the net. That was it.'

The two Helens had much in common. They had both lived in Berkeley, California, the Jacobs family even moving in to one house as the Willses vacated it. They had shared the same coach, William 'Pop' Fuller. They both had fierce concentration on court. But there was such intense rivalry between them that there was no possibility of their being friends and the standard newspaper story accompanying their matches was the long-running one about their 'feud'. In spite of the denials of both women there was always an atmosphere of high tension and drama whenever they met, whether on court or merely in the corridor at Wimbledon. Helen Jacobs to this day insists, 'There was no feud. We certainly weren't close friends or anything like that but we never had an unpleasant word in our lives.'

This may be because they hardly ever spoke any word to each other in their lives. Even when they were escorted out for their finals matches they each acted as if the other wasn't there, Helen Wills just ignoring Helen Jacobs' presence altogether and Helen Jacobs usually plunging promptly into conversation with anyone who happened to be in the vicinity. Norah Gordon Cleather, a sharp observer of Wimbledon psychology, noted, 'Helen Wills' court manners were always perfection, but when she played Helen Jacobs, the veneer always seemed to me to crack a little.'

Miss Cleather considered that the real reason for the distance between them was that they came from different social backgrounds. In fact they were both from comfortable middle-class professional families. Helen Wills's father was a doctor,

while Helen Jacobs' father was in newspaper management for most of his life.

But they did have very different social and personal styles. Helen Wills, nicknamed 'Queen Helen' by the press, presented an imperial front to the world, all cut glass and gold even in her dressing case, Paris haute couture fashions, sophisticated friends in the highest social and artistic circles. She was known as a great beauty, as much perhaps for her regal carriage as for her features. Norah Gordon Cleather, herself a beautiful woman, subjected Helen Wills to careful scrutiny. 'Her features were perfect, her skin flawless, but it was her technique when talking to me that made me realise that she had become one of the loveliest women in the world. It was the technique used by Marlene Dietrich – a trick of choosing

exactly the right moment to look you full in the eyes.

'Only a woman with very beautiful eyes can use that technique effectively, but the result is completely dazzling. It was so in the case of Helen Wills. Afterwards I used to watch her when in conversation with anyone she wished to impress. At exactly the right moment she would turn her face and look her companion suddenly in the eyes. He would invariably stop whatever he was saying, stutter, gaze with his mouth open and forget to shut it until Helen had turned off the charm.'

Miss Cleather seems to have actually liked Helen Jacobs better, portraying her as a 'great mixer, always popular with everyone'. Certainly her press nickname, 'Little Helen', was a much more affectionate title than the other Helen's. A great fighter on court, Helen Jacobs

From the left: **Cilli Aussem** (*left*), **champion in 1931. She beat Mlle Payot of Switzerland in the quarter finals. Helen Wills on her way to victory over Helen Jacobs in the 1932 final. Dorothy Round, the last British woman to win Wimbledon twice with Fraulein Krahwinkel (later Frau Sperling), and in the background, referee F.R. Burrow.** *Below:* **Helen Jacobs finally achieved her ambition of winning Wimbledon in 1936.**

always had the Wimbledon crowd behind her in her battles with Helen Wills. There was more to it, though, than just the traditional British love of an underdog. The crowds never really liked Helen Wills and in all her years at Wimbledon there was not one time when they were really on her side. They always wanted her opponent to win, for one reason or another.

They wanted Lilli de Alvarez, the spectacular Spanish beauty who took everything on the half volley, to win because she excited them with her boldness. Then there was the much-loved Elizabeth 'Chop and Drop' Ryan, eternally unlucky in singles though the most successful doubles player in the history of women's tennis. And of course there was the great British hope, Dorothy Round, who actually took a set off her in 1933, a genuinely thrilling

Helen Wills was presented at court in 1929. Her gown was by Patou. *Opposite:* street chic. *Top right:* Helen with some of her sketches before an exhibition of her work held in a Bond Street gallery. *Below right:* tennis's associations with cigarette advertising predated the Virginia Slims circuit by nearly fifty years.

achievement. The weight of mass dislike is difficult to deal with, as John McEnroe found in his early career, but, fortunately for her, Helen Wills Moody's concentration was so complete she probably didn't notice the crowd reaction.

The values of the day were very different from our own. Then the sport was supposedly amateur, though players were rumoured to receive gifts of money, jewellery, designer clothes, and even cars. The professionalism of Mrs Moody's court attitude, her devotion to being a winner were condemned where we would admire them. Her killer instinct, which we would take for strength of character, was noted with distaste. James R. Harrison of the *New York Morning Telegraph* warned her not to 'high-hat' her public. 'Unless we misread her attitude grossly, the talented Helen has made it plain that the public is a lot of low, common folk whose plaudits do not matter at all.'

The plaudits of others seem to have mattered less to Helen Wills Moody than to any other champion in history, obsessed as she was with her own vision of perfection and possibly sporting immortality. But she was hurt by the criticism of W. O. McGeeham in *The Herald Tribune*, that she did not seem to 'feel the joy of playing'. She was always utterly wrapped up in it when she played, giving herself to the act of hitting the ball over the net as completely as anyone has ever done. It seems doubtful that she could have played as long or as whole-

*Thanks! but I prefer men
with 'Wills of their own'*

heartedly as she did had she not enjoyed the game itself.

But perhaps 'enjoyment' is too mild a word, 'joy' the wrong concept to associate with a woman so driven to achieve, her almost atavistic commitment to dominating her opponent. Helen Wills Moody wanted to be in control. To do that in the dangerous force field of a competitive sport she had to eliminate all distractions, such as crowd noise, linesmen's decisions, even her own choices. She had also to impose her will on the person across the net from her, making that player behave as she wanted her to. Her favourite tactics were to draw her opponent deeper until she was so far beyond the baseline or sidelines that Helen Wills had virtually an open court for her crosscourt winner.

Tennis, for her, was an act of imposing her will, which may have made it hard for her to accept defeat when it came about through circumstances outside her own control. The bitterest match of her career was the 1933 U S final against Helen Jacobs, when at 0–3 down in the third set, she defaulted, an act which scandalised the spectators in much the same way as Roberto Duran's default to Sugar Ray Leonard shocked modern boxing audiences. Duran and Wills, at opposite extremes culturally and emotionally, both had a fierce pride of performance which depended on their cowing their opponents into submission.

That pride could not take undeserved humiliation. Duran walked away from cheap jibes and taunting that should have had no place in a sports arena. Wills's defection was more complicated but probably had a similar motive. She was suffering from a back injury which later required an operation and seemed unable to take being beaten for something that was not her fault.

It wasn't that she simply could not

take being beaten, though Alice Marble recalls playing a practice game with her when they were both on the Wightman Cup team. Alice won the first set and Helen Wills just walked away, without saying a word. 'That's typical Helen, actually,' says C. M. Jones, the tennis writer who

Autograph hunters, packed crowds and long queues are not the prerogative of the modern era.

was himself a fine doubles player. 'She was a terribly difficult person to get on with. I played her in practice at Beckenham once. I never got a single word, not a good afternoon when we started, not a thank you at the end. We just started and hit the ball and played shots. It was kind of eerie. She was such an iceberg, such a one on her own.'

So much on her own was she that at the end of that match in 1933, when Helen Jacobs laid a hand on her shoulder, asking her if she wanted to rest, she pulled away sharply. She may simply have disliked Helen Jacobs, for whatever reason. She may simply have disliked having someone enter her personal territory uninvited. It was safer to stay in the space capsule, remote from human considerations, untouched by the wishes of the other woman.

Above: **Helen Jacobs was the first woman to wear shorts at Wimbledon.** *Below:* **Wills and Jacobs in their 1935 Wimbledon final.** *Opposite:* **Helen, cool as ever, poses for a publicity still.**

That is exactly what she did in 1938, in the last match she played against Helen Jacobs and the reverse image of the 1933 match. Helen Jacobs had not been fit that year and came on court wearing a bandage on her ankle. In the first set games went to four all, when suddenly Helen Jacobs, within a point of taking the next game, twisted to reach a passing shot and landed awkwardly. From then on she could hardly move at all, but she limped doggedly through the rest of the match, determined not to deny Helen Wills a definite victory, as she had been denied hers.

The games mounted for Helen Wills, one after another, as the crowd grew more and more silent, sombre in the face of her remorseless concentration and Helen Jacobs' obvious pain. If Mrs Moody noticed her opponent's injury she gave no

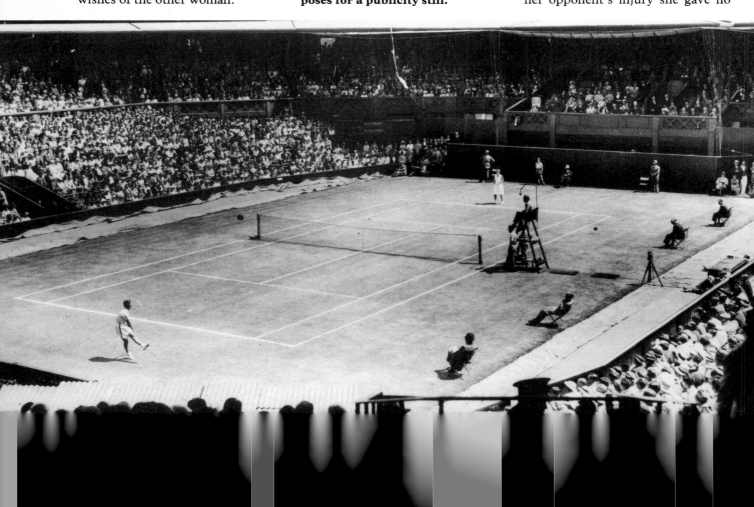

Helen Wills Moody being forced into unexpected athleticism by the imaginative play of Kay Stammers in 1938. The British woman had defeated her at Beckenham in 1935, but her victory was an isolated one. Nobody beat Helen Wills Moody twice.

sign of it. Cold, merciless, she powered her way through game after game, seemingly uncaring. But then no one ever knew what she felt. Perhaps her smile on reaching match point was simply one of relief.

The applause at the end was discreet. Her unique feat of eight Wimbledon singles titles and only one match lost in a fifteen year career there, was met with muted enthusiasm, not the rapturous reception it would have received in other circumstances.

And perhaps it was her own fault but it seems a little sad that so great a champion should have been so unappreciated. From her own books she seems to have been a generous woman with a creative and deeply spiritual nature. But it was one she could not express in public. She appeared cold and repressed when inside she was emotional and romantic. Her first husband, Freddie Moody, was apparently a serious young businessman, but what Helen Wills loved about him was his sense of adventure. He had been all round the world as a seaman, and had, she said, had great and dangerous adventures. He had been attacked by wild-eyed Chileans. He had had his hand bitten through by a Chinaman. Most curious of all, perhaps, given Helen's own orthodox taste, was that he had been tattooed. When she eventually divorced him, she married another dashing figure, Aidan Roark the polo player.

But she could never allow *herself* to appear dashing or romantic. Perhaps she was afraid of appearing unconventional, somehow not respectable. Perhaps she was merely shy. After her encounter with George Bernard Shaw he sent her a copy of his *Saint Joan* with the words, 'Dear Helen Wills, I promised you this at Cliveden. You may remember stealing my heart on that occasion.' And he was not normally an unperspicacious man.

Hilde Sperling in 1936.

5

Not a Killer at All

HILDE SPERLING could drain the blood out of any opponent. She was an excessively elongated woman, tall and thin, with great long legs that helped her run everything down and long arms that shot out, tentacle-like, to trap the ball on her racquet. Her long elegant features remained utterly impassive as she perpetrated slow torture on her opponents. Helen Wills Moody once said she was the hardest of all competitors to play against.

Alice Marble beat her 6–0, 6–0 in the 1939 Wimbledon semi-finals. The match lasted barely twenty minutes.

In the dressing room after, Hilde sat down and began to cry. She was humiliated. Nobody had ever done that to her before. Alice sat down too and began to cry with her.

As sweet-natured as she was in her personal life, on court Alice Marble was the most complete attacking player the women's game had ever seen. She had a fluid, powerful serve, blazingly fast volleys, crushing speed on her groundstrokes, and was faster round the court than any other woman of her time. The thing most commonly said of her was that she played like a man. This meant that she played well.

Throughout the years, when tennis critics have wanted to praise the power or aggression of a woman's play they have said it is like a man's. There have always been women who could volley, right from the very earliest years of the women's game. And they have always been said to have almost masculine strokes or to play the masculine game. What was different about Alice Marble was that, although she was an all court player and happy at the baseline, she built her game around attack and her greatest strengths were her serve and volley. The great women volleyers who have followed her since – Brough and Du Pont, Margaret Court and Billie Jean King, and now Martina Navratilova – have proved that Alice was no freak, and that volleying is not the prerogative of either sex. Alice Marble didn't play like a man. She played like a woman, a fast, graceful, supremely athletic woman.

From childhood onwards she had always been interested in sport. At thirteen she was the mascot for the San Francisco Seals, a Pacific Coast

League baseball team, who picked up on her natural ease of movement and hand-eye co-ordination. She played seven sports at high school before finally settling on tennis, a choice forced on her by her brother Dan, who had worked hard to support the family of five after their father died. Alice was five foot seven inches tall and weighed one hundred and fifty pounds and Dan told her that at fifteen she was too old to be a tomboy. Tennis was a lady-like game, he thought. Alice thought it was silly and sissy and was mortified the first day she had to take her tennis racquet into school.

Her family was a very close and supportive one but it was not a rich one, and tennis in the twenties and thirties was very much a middle-class sport. To get the top class competition they needed to improve, Californians like Alice were sent on playing trips, but the expenses they were given covered only accommodation and travelling for the trip, not the ten blouses and shorts they'd need – nor the three evening dresses. Alice's first tour, to the Northwest and Canadian championships in 1930, was only made possible by the generosity of an unknown benefactor who sent her some money through the post.

One of those playing trips, though, almost ended her career before it had got fully underway. In 1933, in the final qualifying tournament before the American Wightman Cup team was chosen, Alice was asked to play not only in the singles event but to partner the great Helen Wills Moody in the doubles. It was a scorchingly hot day, over a hundred degrees, and she was on court almost continuously from just after ten in the morning until seven in the evening. She played 108 games in five matches, the doubles being particularly strenuous as Mrs Moody had an injured back and left all the overheads for her. Later that summer Mrs Moody was to make her notorious default to Helen Jacobs in the U S Open final, but Alice Marble didn't allow herself the

Left: **Alice Marble with some teenage fans at Surbiton.**
Above: **Alice's first Wimbledon after her recovery from severe illness, 1937. She found time to spectate too** (*right*).

luxury of withdrawing. She lost twelve pounds that day and collapsed later in the evening suffering from sunstroke and anaemia.

Throughout the following winter and spring she felt low, but it wasn't until the French Open the following year, 1934, that she realised the full extent of the damage her longest day had done. She collapsed on court against Madame Sylvia Henrotin and had to be rushed to hospital.

When she was finally brought home to the States the doctors told her she had tuberculosis and would never play tennis again. It was to be two years before she proved them wrong, two years of illness, physical weakness and despair that she would ever be well again.

Her coach at that time was Eleanor 'Teach' Tennant, possessive and domineering but one of the finest motivators as a coach that the game has known. Years later she was to bring Maureen Connolly to stardom too. Teach took over Alice's life, paying the bill for her to stay in a sanatorium in the sunny climate of Southern California, and encouraging her in her recovery when Alice finally decided she could stand the sanatorium no longer. Teach's willingness to take control helped Alice through her illness, though in later

In 1937 (*above*) **Alice was beaten in the quarter final, but in 1938 (*right*) she reached the semi-final, only to be defeated by fellow American Helen Jacobs, 6–4 6–4.**

Alice's cause through her illness, Marlene Dietrich, Jeanette Mac-Donald, Robert Taylor. The two were invited too to the Hearst ranch at San Simeon, where the dining room had been constructed from the interior of an Italian church and at Christmas the guests were invited into a room like a department store to choose their own presents. One visit to San Simeon drew forth a lyrical tribute from Arthur Brisbane, the Hearst columnist:

'What a girl Alice Marble is, with everything the Venus de Milo has, plus two muscular, bare, sunburned arms marvellously efficient. Her legs are like two columns of polished mahogany, bare to the knees, her figure perfect. Frederick MacMennies should do a statue of her. And she should marry the most intelligent young man in America, and be the perfect mother, with twelve children, not merely the world's best tennis player, which she probably will be.'

She never did have the twelve children. Her one marriage was brief, only three short years of happiness before her husband was killed in the war. It was a marriage she couldn't even admit in public as he was in intelligence work. But she did become the world's best tennis player, a class above the rest in her attitude and technique. 'She was the most professional of them all,' remembers Kay Stammers, the British Wightman Cup player. 'Nobody else had a pro who came everywhere like Teach Tennant did with her. There was a man who trailed along all the time too so that Alice could hit with a man.' Such dedication brought Alice the Wimbledon mixed in 1937, the mixed and the women's doubles in 1938, and all three titles in 1939.

1939, the last uncertain summer before Europe plunged yet again into the misery of war. Alice had

years it was to cause them to split. When Alice turned pro she shared her income fifty-fifty with Teach for three years before the break. 'When I got to twenty-six or twenty-seven I wanted to go out and study and do things,' says Alice today. 'But she was an enormously possessive woman. I wanted to have a life of my own so we split up. But we got together again later on and got to be friends.'

It was Teach who introduced Alice to the glamorous side of tennis, through the stars she coached – Carole Lombard, who championed

Right: **Alice Marble's opponent in the 1939 final was Britain's popular Kay Stammers, pictured left and above. Even in the forties the British could not compete with the American facilities and climate. 'We all had Dan Maskell at Wimbledon as our coach, for an hour or two twice a week,' recalls Kay. 'Half the time you'd go plodding down there and there'd be frost on the court or it'd be raining. It was quite hard work just getting the practice.'**

twice won the U S National Championships and was favourite for the Wimbledon title, though the Lawn Tennis Correspondent of *The Times* felt that, 'Like all the others, except Mrs Moody, we have seen that there comes a day when her game goes to pieces, and over a fortnight's play the Wimbledon Championship is more likely to be won by strong nerves than strokes.'

In the event Alice's matches were so one sided she hardly needed strong nerves. Even in the final against Kay Stammers, an imaginative and daring shotmaker with her home crowd behind her, she conceded only two games. C. M. Jones, one of Britain's leading scholars of the game, has revealed the astonishing fact that Kay Stammers hit more winners than errors in that match, a performance that no woman since has equalled in the final. That it did not win her the 1939 final indicates the almost flawless tennis Alice Marble played that day.

'What with the wind and the showers of a grey day and the hopeless massacre of a match that some people had stayed up all night to watch, I have never before seen the Centre Court so unmoved,' said *The Times* man, his patriotic hopes of a British victory thwarted. He may have misread the atmosphere. Alice's stunning tennis, so bold and free and graceful, fired the imaginations of a whole generation of American women and disarmed the male spectators.

John Olliff, the *Daily Telegraph*'s tennis writer, wrote of her,

'There was a time when I used to think that a girl's job was to sit and look pretty, and athletics should be left to the hardier sex. But I left school soon afterwards and began to realise that it depends entirely on the girl. Alice Marble was obviously intended to do exactly what she does.

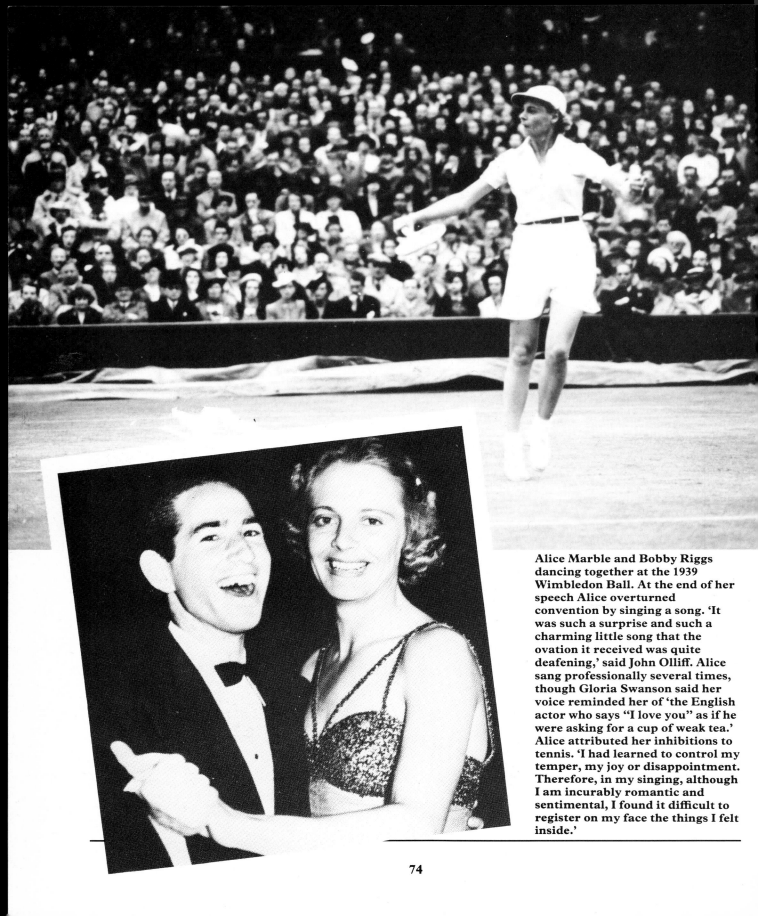

Alice Marble and Bobby Riggs dancing together at the 1939 Wimbledon Ball. At the end of her speech Alice overturned convention by singing a song. 'It was such a surprise and such a charming little song that the ovation it received was quite deafening,' said John Olliff. Alice sang professionally several times, though Gloria Swanson said her voice reminded her of 'the English actor who says "I love you" as if he were asking for a cup of weak tea.' Alice attributed her inhibitions to tennis. 'I had learned to control my temper, my joy or disappointment. Therefore, in my singing, although I am incurably romantic and sentimental, I found it difficult to register on my face the things I felt inside.'

She plays tennis like a very gifted and athletic man, and adds grace and beauty of form into the bargain.'

Like the most memorable – though not always the greatest – of champions, she created a feeling of excitement in those who watched her. She was beautiful and statuesque – and blonde – and played with a magnificently powerful elegance. But more than that she played with joy, an uninhibited love of what she was doing that was not seen again in a top class player until the arrival of Evonne Goolagong.

Alice's game, though, was more purposeful than the sunny Australian's. Her long struggle against illness forged her into a champion. She had always loved competing, loved just taking part, but she had been, said Teach Tennant, 'Basically not a fighter. She did not have in her ten cents worth of fight. Not a killer at all. Alice does not like me saying this at all.'

At seventy Alice can look back and recognise, 'I didn't have the will to win for a long while. Winning didn't seem so important. I just enjoyed it. Later I felt I had to win because it was so important to all the people who'd helped me so much – Teach, my family. I really wanted to win for them.'

The move from her simple love of competing to a real desire to win was achieved with the help of Teach's usual psychological manipulation. At that time she was also coaching Bobby Riggs, the man who will probably be remembered more for his defeat to Billie Jean King at the Astrodome than for his triple crown at Wimbledon. Riggs was cocky to the point of arrogance, and Teach intensified the natural rivalry of the two potential champions. 'I'd say, "Well Bobby Riggs sure played tennis out of this world yesterday." Or to Bobby I'd say, "Alice Marble could sure take you." And it always

stimulated their adrenalin gland and their practising together – the two of them – was very helpful. Bobby's arrogant attitude towards Alice stimulated her as well.'

Both Riggs and Alice Marble took three titles each at the 1939 Wimbledon, as remarkable a triumph for the woman pitting them together in the background as for the players themselves. The irony was that for all

In 1939 Alice also won the Kent Championship, played at Beckenham.

A typical publicity shot of Alice Marble on board a transatlantic liner. She used to get five hundred letters a week when the U S Championships were on, many from people wanting to be champions. 'Then there were crank letters, mostly either mash notes or abusive ones. Abuse is more direct too. If I didn't play well, or lost a match, the public was often violent. Spectators would grab me by the arm and say, "I came out for a good day and you ruined it for me." They did everything but hit me. This happens to every public character.'

Riggs's male arrogance, it was Alice who was the attacking player, he the tortuous baseliner given to long rallies and late taken balls. Where Alice Marble opened up a whole new era of power tennis for women, Bobby Riggs was said 'to have turned a complete cycle back to the principles of the Dohertys, and later on Lacoste and Austin'. Even in his own age Riggs was an anachronism. How could he have hoped to survive in Billie Jean's?

As the championships of 1939 ended, the usual London sales were in full swing but the advertisement drawings of shantung morning wrappers were next to photographs of Wellington bombers being constructed in Weybridge. Alice Marble was never to play at Wimbledon again, but seven years later, when the war was over and she herself was a professional, it was almost as if she had never been away. There was a whole generation of serving, volleying, smashing young women. Alice's game had not been forgotten.

Now after a life time of lung illnesses and five operations for cancer in the last few months she still plays tennis socially and has a part time job at a local club in Palm Desert. 'I never had a chance to play sudden death. I would have enjoyed that. When we play that now I just get a kick out of it. I think I would have been quite good at it,' she says gleefully.

6

The New Wave

BRITAIN WAS NO LONGER as it had been. It was not quite its old self, not yet its new. There was rubble in streets where there had once been houses, signs of bombing everywhere. Even Wimbledon had not escaped. The roof of the club toolhouse had been demolished and part of the north east entrance. And you could still see the bomb damage on the Centre Court, where twelve hundred seats had been destroyed by a five hundred pounder. But there was a longing in the country for the new: new ways of life, new houses, new ideas. A new government had been elected the year before, in 1945, the airport at Heathrow was new – and the first plane that landed there from America brought a new race of women tennis players.

None of the women on the 1946 American Wightman Cup team had ever been abroad before. But Pauline Betz, Margaret Osborne, Louise Brough and Doris Hart had waited a long time for the moment when they would step off that plane and land in Britain, home of Wimbledon. All through the war they had plugged away at their tennis, playing in patriotic tournaments and their national championships at Forest Hills. But Wimbledon was the tournament they had dreamed of and been denied, the world's championship set in a quiet English suburb. They were excited, as British crowds would be by them.

The British had thought their own Wightman Cup team as good as any. Lance Tingay, remembers looking forward to the competition

Above left: **Pat Todd, Louise Brough, Pauline Betz, Dodo Bundy (daughter of May Sutton Bundy), Margaret Osborne and Doris Hart.**
Above: **Arriving in London, Margaret Osborne, Doris Hart and Louise Brough.**

The 1946 Wimbledon went on in spite of bomb damage on the Centre Court (*far left*).

Left: **Pauline Betz, the 1946 champion, receiving her trophy from Queen Mary, with Lord Louis and Lady Edwina Mountbatten in attendance. Her opponent was Louise Brough** (*below right*) **who appeared in seven Wimbledon finals, winning four of them. Pauline also won the US Championship in the same year** (*below*).

with patriotic confidence. 'We all wrote pieces saying we'd win,' he says. 'We thought we had two jolly good players in Kay Stammers, who was the finalist to Alice Marble just before the war, and Jean Bostock, who was an absolute genius. Then along came the Wightman Cup and everybody was absolutely flabbergasted by the standard. Doris Hart, who won Wimbledon in 1951, was so below the standard of the others that she couldn't play a single.'

They were straightforward, ruthless, efficient, these four, with their powerful men's games and their simple, practical clothes. They all wore plain shorts and shirts, mostly home-made, because there hadn't been any tennis dresses to buy during the war. To the British women they seemed 'as strong as oxes,' remembers Kay Stammers, now Mrs Bullitt. 'There we were, rather emaciated married women and mothers. The reason why we had to struggle away was because there was nobody

in England coming on. That's why we had to hold the fort as best we could. It was hard work. I'm afraid by that time the American girls were very much better than we were. They played a stronger game. They really were very very good.'

The British didn't win a match in the Wightman Cup and by that time it was obvious there would be an American champion at Wimbledon. Like the other Europeans, the British had played no competitive tennis at all during the war and Wimbledon itself had been commandeered by troops, its quiet reading room turned into a dormitory

Pauline Betz and an admirer in 1946.
Above: **Louise Brough in action.**

fitted with iron bedsteads, the Grand Walk outside the clubhouse transformed into a parade ground, where shrieks and yells from bayonet practice often rang out. Norah Gordon Cleather, the assistant secretary, had even kept pigs in one of the car parks.

The Americans could not have seemed more fabulous creatures to the natives had their plane dropped them among some primitive tribe in the Brazilian rain forest. All of them, even baseliner Pauline Betz, played power tennis, hitting out at the ball with uninhibited strength and running and jumping as freely, if not

perhaps as gracefully, as the great Alice Marble had done seven years before. That one country should produce four such stars at once seemed a success of fantastic proportions, though in fact they were really of two generations, Betz and Osborne about five years older than the other pair.

In 1946 Pauline Betz was the acknowledged champion, a three time winner of the US Nationals, which in the absence of anything else were as close as anyone got to a world championship during the war. Betz was a 'clutch' player, the one who could pull something extra out of her wide repertoire of shots when a match got tough. She 'makes wonderful use of variety and surprise,' said Sarah Palfrey Cooke, one of the

best doubles players of her day and a two time member of the US nationals herself, both times against Pauline Betz. 'How well she seems to know when to change the pace, when to hit a soft serve and when a hard one.' She was afraid of no one, never once stepped on a court thinking she'd lose, even when, as a youngster, she came up against Alice Marble, the then champion.

Unlike the other post-war stars she had not modelled her game on Marble's, did not play the big serve and volley game. But the link between the two generations was there in that she had been coached for a time by Teach Tennant. 'She was quite an unusual person,' Pauline remembers. 'She didn't work on the game so much as she worked on the

personality. She used to give you pep talks like a football coach. But I was sort of a rebel as far as anyone taking over my life and running it was concerned and I never got involved.'

Witty, cultured, charming, Pauline Betz was a highly educated woman who just happened to be obsessed by tennis. She never refused a tournament anywhere, travelling all over north America, to Florida, the Eastern grass court circuit, even Puerto Rica and Guiana on a government sponsored tour where she played inside aeroplane hangars, on basketball pitches and even once on a court where the only lights came from jeeps lined up round the court with their headlights on.

Such dedication and industry

took her to the top in a sport which still retained much of its light-hearted atmosphere in many ways. Even at the top levels of the game in Britain, Kay Stammers remembers, 'If somebody hit a good shot we said, "Good shot!" Or if they just missed we said, "Bad luck!" You'd never hear anything like that today!' Pauline Betz herself remembers once hearing a woman at the Beverly Hills Tennis Club say, 'I'd have reached it if I'd walked faster.'

Her approach, while she tried to keep it instinctive, was considerably more serious than that. At fourteen she was already working hard trying to make her backhand like Don Budge's, with the way 'his entire body seemed to flow right into the shot.' She succeeded, making her backhand one of the most feared strokes in the women's game, though her tactical ability was just as formidable a weapon. John Olliff thought her one of the most intelligent players he had ever seen, equalled only by Norman Brookes and Bobby Riggs.

As expected she won the 1946 Wimbledon on what was to be her first and last attempt. Later that year she lost her amateur status, not for taking money or signing a professional contract – but for enquiring about the possibility of professional dates at a number of clubs. Betz had, in any case, lost much of her motivation to continue in tournament play after winning Wimbledon, but she was bitter about being forced into professionalism, particularly as the top men had always made sure their plans to turn pro were well publicised beforehand. Now, thirty five years on, she is pleased about the amounts of money the women can make today, especially when their earnings top those of the men.

Louise Brough (*left*) **and Margaret Osborne DuPont – close friends off court and fierce rivals on it.**

In her time the men took the lion's share both of the money and of the audiences in the amateur as well as the professional game. Women pros had to rely on their novelty value. Pauline Betz used to dress in ridiculous costumes and give comic instructional clinics before her matches. Later, when 'Gorgeous Gussy' Moran of lace panties fame turned professional, Pauline kicked off their tour in Madison Square Garden wearing leopardskin shorts.

In 1947 there were plenty of contenders for her place at the top of the amateur game. Margaret Osborne, with her fine American twist serve and devastating volleying was first to take over the Wimbledon title, defeating Doris Hart in the 1947 final. Dark haired and shy, Margaret's quiet, reserved nature off court belied her competitiveness on it. So determined was she that Helen Jacobs, who had recognised her championship potential when she was only thirteen, commented, 'one couldn't help but wonder if she would ever be willing to sacrifice attack for defence when defence became strategically wise. That a strong defence can be the best offensive was a tennis axiom of which Margaret had apparently never heard.'

But then Margaret's greatest rival was another woman who loved to attack, Louise Brough, perhaps the most underrated champion of all who won not only the singles in three successive Wimbledons – 1948, 1949 and 1950 – but also five out of the six doubles titles in those years. She won nine ladies and mixed doubles titles at Wimbledon alone and recaptured the singles in 1955, after Maureen Connolly's tragic accident put her out of tennis for good.

Tall and very powerful, she had a fine serve, not perhaps as consistent as that of Margaret Osborne – who was thought to make less service faults than any woman since Suzanne Lenglen – but just as strong. She was a superb volleyer and had one of the most varied of games, 'a different type of game from most people,' remembers Bea Seal, current umpire and former player. 'She was what I call a cutter and carver. She put a tremendous amount of slice on the ball. She played tennis rather like the shots in real tennis, where everything is cut. She never really played a straight ball. The others played in a more straightforward way and she messed them up with her game.'

She and Margaret Osborne were always together, friends off court and the most devastating doubles partnership ever seen in the women's game on it. Even now they are still talked of in the same breath, bracketed together as equals – and indeed they were equals, Louise's triple Wimbledon being matched by Margaret's three successive US titles in the same years. They were the democratic champions, with no aura of invincibility or cult of personality built around them. Teddy Tinling, who prefers his stars to behave like stars, described finding them once playing together, completely unnoticed on Court 12 at Queen's Club. 'Helen Wills's presence would have been sensed by everyone in the club,' he noted disapprovingly.

But inseparable as they were they found not the slightest contradiction in facing each other across the net, though people invariably thought they would find it difficult to play each other. 'That used to make us so mad,' remembers Margaret. 'As hard as we fought to win the doubles together we were both equally anxious to win the singles and it didn't matter who we were playing. We fought just as hard when we were playing each other. Whichever one of us won, the other was glad for

her – but we really wanted to win ourselves.'

They were the greatest players of their day whether singly or together, and the only person to approach them in skill – though not in achievement – was Doris Hart, who won Wimbledon in 1951 but was more often a runner up in singles than a winner. A smooth, graceful

Gussy Moran modelling a Balmain creation at the Dorchester Hotel.

strokemaker with a fine serve and the most delicate touch, especially on her dropshots, Doris thrilled spectators by the aesthetic quality of her tennis rather than its robustness. The way she played was beautiful. She gave people an image to take away and remember, even when she did not win.

That she could compete at all was

The professional game had rather different sartorial requirements than those of Wimbledon. Pauline Betz matched Gussy's leopardskin with gold lamé shorts when they played at Madison Square Garden in 1950.

due to her courage and rare natural talent. Never did a child have so many ailments – chicken pox, scarlet fever, a mastoid operation, a bilateral hernia and double pneumonia as well as the most serious of all, a poisoned leg that left her with a permanent limp and impaired her mobility round the court. She compensated partly by her superb anticipation, but she was neither as strong nor as consistent as Margaret and Louise. 'I would think, playing as hard as they do today, it's doubtful whether she could stand the pace,' comments Kay Stammers. 'They've got to be terribly strong now because they train like crazy.'

Betz, Brough, Osborne and Hart trained like crazy too, but they did not have the constant matchplay that the modern women have, the travelling, the frenetic pace. 'I think we had a very much better time,' says Kay Stammers. 'We met so many people. We had fun. We weren't dashing all over the world. If you did go anywhere it was in a boat so it wasn't much of a dash.'

But they were pioneers, these four great Americans, so dedicated to their sport that they considered nothing but tennis and left room for nothing else in their lives. Only Margaret Osborne married while she was still playing, becoming the wife of millionaire William DuPont in 1948. When she had her son in 1952 her days as a serious challenger for the singles title were over, though she had a last brief burst of glory in 1962, when she won the mixed with Neale Fraser at the age of forty-four. Louise Brough reckons that there was only one choice. 'We didn't think about getting married. Marriage isn't such a big deal anyway,' she says. 'I knew lots of people who married at twenty-one or twenty-two and it didn't work out. Or maybe they were just meant to be housewives.'

Above left: **Doris Hart, a popular winner and a great stylist, receiving her trophy for winning the 1951 Wimbledon from Princess Marina of Kent. Doris was one of the most elegant and fluid strokemakers of all time, but a childhood illness had left her with a damaged leg, which was said to impair her mobility. Her contemporary, Pauline Betz, disagrees. 'She moved pretty well,' she says laconically. 'Her anticipation was so good it didn't matter.'**

Louise Brough was not. She would have been an ideal professional in today's world, utterly dedicated, an indefatigable competitor, and completely lacking in the arrogance that has emerged in some players as the game has mushroomed. And competing so often she would not perhaps have suffered the crippling nervousness that struck her later on in her career, when she would throw the ball up three or four or five times before being able to serve. Maureen Connolly, who beat her twice at Wimbledon, said,

'I often thought she beat herself through nervousness. She's highstrung and there was the added pressure of knowing there had been a better, brighter day in her career.'

The two never met on equal terms. When Maureen was at her peak, Louise was nearly thirty, the gap just too great for her to fend off this hungriest of challengers. Looking back across the years she just sighs, 'When you've reached a certain age and this young player comes along and runs you all over the court ... well ... she seemed very great.'

7

The Woman Warrior

Maureen Connolly arriving in London for the first time with her coach, Eleanor 'Teach' Tennant, in 1952.

SHE DIDN'T LOOK GREAT. She looked ordinary. Maureen Connolly had none of the aristocratic hauteur of a Bueno or a Wade, none of the manifest athleticism of a Margaret Court, none of the dramatic emotionalism of a Lenglen. She was, to all outward appearance, a typical fifties teenager, who liked fluffy jumpers and horses and whose favourite tennis dress had silly little poodles embroidered round the edges.

But Maureen Connolly was as great as Louise Brough had sensed she was, one of the most unusual champions the sport of tennis ever had. Underneath that guise of sub-urban normality was a girl who thought of herself as a tennis war-rior. Her raging warrior's spirit won her three Wimbledon, three US, two French and an Australian title and she was the first woman to win the Grand Slam. Her mental con-centration was legendary, but the quality she had was more than just the ability to block out everything but the game in hand. She had a concentrated aggression, an ability

to focus on the ultimate objective of the game – the winning of it – as well as on the individual points along the way. Others have wanted to win as much as she did. Few have needed to win more.

She was short, stocky, unremarkable in appearance, and hardly even looked like an athlete, but the intensity of that need to win, its compulsive quality ranked her with the theatrically glamorous Suzanne Lenglen as one of the most obsessional of tennis champions. Suzanne was a driven creature spurred on by her father, without whom she might not have achieved what she did. Maureen may have achieved what she did because she had no father. Her parents divorced when she was four and she took an immediate dislike to the man her mother later married. As her mother was bent on pushing her daughter into the musical career she had never had herself, tennis was probably Maureen's way of asserting her personality, her emotional needs. Within the tramlines of the tennis court she staked out her territory.

Perhaps because of the insecurity of her home she wanted desperately to be liked. She thought if she won she would be. But, paradoxically, her determination to win made her seem hard and precocious and at Wimbledon at least, despite mass publicity, she never received the popularity her warm personality off the court might have attracted.

At that time too she *was* hard in a way, and perhaps the crowds sensed it. It has become a cliché of sports motivation that competitors should hate their opponents. Few people really do. Most have to psyche themselves up even to approach that

Maureen Connolly, seen (*right*) **signing an autograph (with her *left* hand) for a young admirer, was as friendly off court as she was determined on it.**

feeling. But Maureen Connolly, beneath the healthy teenage image, really did hate her opponents. 'This was no passing dislike,' she wrote, 'but a blazing, virulent, powerful and consuming hate. I believed I could not win without hatred. And win I must because I was afraid to lose.'

There was no mercy in her, no compassion on the tennis court. 'I attacked my weaker opponents more ferociously than any other girl in the history of tennis,' she confessed.

Her very first visit to Wimbledon revealed the tortured ruthlessness that lay at the heart of her game. She was only seventeen, already the winner of the U S Open and the sensation of the 1952 championships before she had ever struck a ball. She injured her shoulder at Queen's just two days before Wimbledon began, setting off a media stampede to find out whether she would play or not.

That question was a crucial one in her relationship with her coach Teach Tennant. Teach, who had

guided Alice Marble to stardom thirteen years previously, had taken over Maureen's coaching when she was only thirteen. According to Maureen, Teach was 'always dominant, outspoken, a positive thinker at all times; she abhorred stupidity, and her likes, dislikes and opinions were considerably less than State secrets.' In this case her opinion was that Maureen would damage her shoulder permanently if she played, while Maureen thought the injury was a minor one. Both had medical support for their views and their disagreement was vehement, in the end bitter.

Teach was one of the most extraordinary motivators ever in tennis, a woman who could convince a player of her invincibility and who used her players' deepest character traits to fashion their success. With Alice Marble those traits had been joy in playing and an earnest desire to repay both Teach and her family

for their support. With Maureen they were darker, more complex, and developed eventually into a destructive force that would turn on Teach herself. 'Teach was the greatest psychologist I think I ever knew,' says Alice Marble. 'She just knew the right things to say. They made a film about Maureen which portrayed Teach as cruel but she was just determined. There's no way I could ever have hated *my* opponents. I just don't have that kind of makeup. You want to go out and beat somebody but not at any cost. But Maureen was that type of player. She was a tiger. She looked like she hated her opponents. I had fun with mine.'

All along Teach Tennant had fed the hatred within the young girl. The year before their dispute at Wimbledon, Maureen had become the youngest player ever to win the US title at Forest Hills, at sixteen a year younger than Helen Wills

Left: **Maureen Connolly after winning the 1952 final, hiding her emotions in her towel.**
Below: **Receiving her trophy from Princess Marina. Louise Brough's emotions are only too obvious.**

Moody. To do so she had had to beat Doris Hart, the Wimbledon champion and the one woman in tennis whom Maureen hero-worshipped. Teach had had her fed the rumour that Doris, for all her superficial friendliness and charm, thought Maureen was a spoiled brat and was out to teach her a tennis lesson. Hurt, disillusionment and flaming hot anger propelled Maureen to the win over Doris which took her to the finals and eventually the title against Shirley Fry.

Now, almost a year later, Maureen was not about to be manipulated again. She had wanted to break with Teach in the past but her mother had always held them together. This time, though, nothing was more important for Maureen than playing at Wimbledon. Even before a third medical opinion confirmed that she could play – she had fibrositis requiring nothing more serious than intensive heat treat-

ment – she had removed the obstacle which stood in her way. Teach Tennant had been ruthless in the means she used to create this most remorseless of champions. 'She was like a Svengali with her pupils,' says Lance Tingay. 'It was as though she was inflicting some horrible mental lesbianism on young people. Maureen must have sensed that unhealthy weight of regard that Teach put into her. She had great strength of character.'

Possibly even Teach did not realise how much. Maureen took the then unprecedented step of calling a press conference to make public her break with her coach. Teach was in Liverpool meeting a friend from the boat and Maureen's mother had temporarily disappeared from the scene as Maureen told the assembled press that Teach no longer represented her views. She would act on her own authority from that time forward. She was still only seven-

Maureen Connolly, always ready to laugh *off* court, was at the height of her powers in 1953, her Grand Slam year, providing food for thought for Doris Hart, who also faced her in the French and US finals that year. Maureen's success was due in great part to her strength of spirit. The day before she died of cancer in 1969 she wrote out a list of books that she wanted her two daughters, Cindy and Brenda, to read. She was under heavy medication and knew she had not long to live.

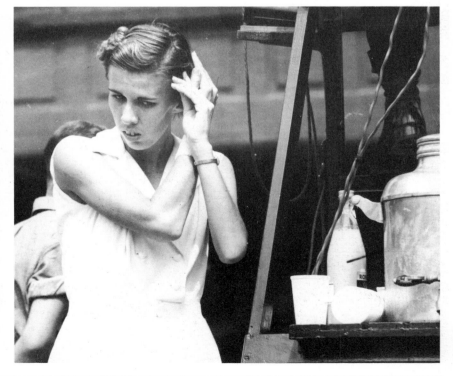

teen. Later Teach was able to understand Maureen's need for independence. 'Boy! I can well remember striking out on my own,' she wrote to her former protégée. 'Your winning without me gives me personal and professional satisfaction.' But inside she was bitterly hurt by Maureen's defection and the two never really became reconciled, as Teach and Alice Marble did. Five years later, after the tragic accident that cut short Maureen's career, the links were severed for the last time with what Teach described as 'a brief phone call, a brief, almost wordless visit, and a cheque for a very small sum left on my dining-room table.'

But in 1952, unaware of the sadness that was later to fall on her, Maureen fought her way to the Wimbledon final – without Teach. She survived a hard fourth round match when the British player Susan Partridge came within two points of beating her. In that moment she knew 'this was my year, this was my hour, this was my time to become a champion.' She was flagging and a young US Air Force boy suddenly shouted into the hushed atmosphere of Wimbledon 'Give 'em hell, Mo!' She did, powering her way through the web of moonballs and lobs that Susan Partridge had spun around her to take that final set and the match. Her moment of inner certainty was no more than the gut feelings Eleanor Tennant would have when she knew one of her players was going to win.

From that moment the 1952 Wimbledon was the beginning of a triumphal march into tennis legend for Maureen Connolly. She beat Shirley Fry and then Louise Brough to take the title that year, proving that her US title the year before had been no fluke. In fact, she was never to be beaten in a Grand Slam event in the few short years she was to play, and only very rarely apart from that. Shirley Fry, the tireless retriever who denied Maureen the pace she thrived on, possibly gave her more trouble than any other player, though Doris Hart twice beat her, once in her Grand Slam year of 1953, in the final of the Italian Championships. Beverly Baker Fleitz, the ambidextrous player with a forehand on both sides, could also stretch her, though was hardly in the same class, never having won a major championship. Few of her contemporaries *were* in the same class. 'She annihilated me when I first played her,' remembers Althea Gibson, though her own game had not then developed into the champion's game it later became. 'Any time a player from the baseline can pass you within a three inch distance she is great. She could pass you through a needle's eye. That's how great a player she was.'

In her whole top class career she had only four defeats, a remarkable record and one which more than anything gives her a claim to be one of the all-time greats. Bea Seal, the British umpire who herself played in the Connolly era, says of her, 'I don't think I can ever recall Maureen making an unforced error. I've seen Martina make unforced errors, very few this year admittedly, but Maureen just never made an error. She had to be beaten on shot. She had an answer to everything. I think she'd have found the answers to Martina.' Lance Tingay, who believes that the supreme woman baseliner will always beat the supreme woman volleyer, agrees with Mrs Seal. 'She would have beaten Margaret Court and Martina Navrati-

Maureen Connolly in 1954, her last year of competitive tennis before the cruel accident that was to end her career.

Left: **The forehand drive that hit her opponent's racquet with the weight of a cricket ball.** *Below:* **The 1954 final was against Louise Brough.** *Right:* **The Wimbledon Ball. Maureen leading out the first waltz with the 1954 men's champion, crowd favourite Jaroslav Drobny.**

lova – certainly. She would have frightened Martina.'

She would have frightened most people who met her across the net, though off court she was a warm, bubbly extrovert with a great sense of fun. She was never a natural volleyer but had already built herself a net game and was in the process of producing the big serve when she had to give up tennis. But although she did not have the so-called attacking game, the serve and volley game, she was very much an attacking player, hitting out for the lines with only the smallest margin of error. After her split with Teach she worked with Harry Hopman, the Australian Davis Cup coach, and his wife Nell, whose 'go for broke' philosophy coincided with the needs of her own competitive temperament.

She was a real exponent of power tennis, enjoying her own physical strength and revelling in her speed around the court, her flashy footwork – she had even practised tap dancing to sharpen the footwork, much to Teach's disapproval. C.M. Jones remembers hitting not only with Maureen Connolly, but with Helen Wills and Alice Marble as well. 'Undoubtedly the weight of the ball when it hit your racquet from both Helen Wills and Maureen Connolly was very heavy. It was as if a cricket ball was hitting your racquet, it was that heavy. They did hit the ball very hard but it was also the result of very good technique. They hit it flat with a very low trajectory. All this topspin today makes it seem like a puffball on the other side.'

Two relentless champions, the older one seeing her own greatness mirrored in the younger. Maureen Connolly once played her in a mixed doubles and did not think she could have beaten the great Helen at her best. 'She had not been practising, her footwork was slow, she made errors. Yet she outguessed me at every turn!' she enthused. But only a tragic accident deprived her of the chance to match Helen's impeccable record. Just two weeks after her third successive Wimbledon victory her right leg was crushed against a speeding truck as her beloved horse, Colonel Merryboy, wheeled away in panic. She never played competitive tennis again.

Had she done so she might have compiled a glittering record. Nothing in sport is ever certain but Maureen Connolly's great, gallant, gutsy temperament would surely not have failed her. It did not fail her after her accident, when she might have been forgiven for bitterness. She married fellow sportsman Norman Brinker, an Olympic horseman, and gave the rest of her short life to her family and to junior tennis. She was only thirty four when she died of cancer.

Through Nell Hopman, who taught her to concentrate her emotions on court in a less self destructive way, she had learned at last to win with love and not hate. In her life after tennis she proved she had learned an even harder lesson, to lose with love and not hate.

Left: **Maureen Connolly with her husband Norman Brinker, himself an Olympic pentathlete. Maureen covered Wimbledon for a Fleet Street newspaper when her own career was over and used to bring her husband into the press room. Lance Tingay remembers them holding hands under the table as Maureen wrote her articles.**

Below left: **Shirley Fry winning the 1956 final against Britain's Angela Buxton. Shirley was often forgotten amongst her more brilliant contemporaries but she was a dogged competitor and a great doubles player, winning four US, four French, and three Wimbledon ladies doubles championships with Doris Hart.**

Below right: **Louise Brough winning the title which gave her more satisfaction than any other in her career, the 1955 Wimbledon final against ambidextrous Beverly Baker Fleitz, seven years her junior.**

8

The Reluctant Ambassador

IT WAS FASHIONABLE to be an outsider in the fifties. You existed
on coffee and cigarettes,which you consumed inside smokey jazz
clubs, and your main item of dress was a black polo neck jumper.
You admired bohemians, the homeless and rebels against society,
though you were too busy reading about all these people in
existentialist novels to do any rebelling yourself. Althea Gibson too
was an outsider in the 1950s, but she did it the unfashionable way.
She was black.

This woman, one of the finest
natural athletes that tennis has ever
seen, was the first black person of
either sex to win a Wimbledon
singles title. She was fast, fiery, powerful, and uninhibitedly aggressive
in going for her shots, yet for all her
obvious talents it took many years
for her to mature as a player. Women
from socially acceptable middle-
class homes could afford to work
their way up the rankings by playing
the amateur circuit.

Althea Gibson needed something
more solid than sport to survive in
an Anglo-Saxon world. She was always going to have to make a life for
herself after tennis, and the streets
of Harlem had prepared her only for
life on the streets of Harlem. The
years she might have spent estab-
lishing herself and her game had she

been from a safer, more prosperous
class, went on acquiring herself an
education, a commodity Althea had
had little respect for when it was
offered her first time around. The
game she had played most at school
had always been hookey.

Class . . . It's one of the unknowns
in sport, hard to say how much part
it plays in success. With some
sportsmen – boxers and Billie Jean
King in particular – it's a strong mo-
tivating force, driving them on to
achieve the social and economic status they feel they've been denied.
But it doesn't follow that all rich kids
are going to be losers.

*People would always say to me you
had to be hungry to succeed and that
as I came from an upper-middle class*

background there was no way I would have the driving force. Billie Jean would say that of me I think. She felt hardships in her childhood because she did not come from an upper class background and tennis was quite an upper class sport in America then. I always thought it was a lot of rubbish when people said that about me because I had a force within me that would not allow me to do otherwise.

Althea Gibson did everything for herself too. It was almost as if she was an outsider in her own family. Of all of them, three sisters and a brother, she was the only one who was ever in trouble. The energy and aggression that she later channelled into hitting hell out of a tennis ball went into basketball in the gymnasium or the park, on running away when she'd stolen soft fruit from the freight cars at the market, on fist fights with the other tough kids trying to stand up for themselves on the streets of Harlem.

At twelve Althea was so big and strong and brave that her father wanted her to be a prize fighter. Women's boxing was later made illegal, not that Althea had any fluttery feminine misgivings about the sport. 'I could fight,' she said. 'Daddy taught me the moves, and I

Above left: **Althea Gibson on her first visit to Britain in 1951, seen through the lens of** *Picture Post* **photographer Bert Hardy. An outsider looking in at Wimbledon?** *Below left:* **Althea winning the Surrey championship in the same year.**

Above: **Althea at Beckenham. She was isolated, said Teddy Tinling. 'She could never find doubles partners of her own high standard and even in Europe I have seen her compatriots move off when she approached.'**

had the right temperament for it. I was tough. I wasn't afraid of anybody, not even him,' – despite the fact that he used to beat her with a strap and once even punched her in the face when she hadn't come home for a couple of nights.

Tennis gave Althea Gibson a discipline she had never had before. Wild and lawless, she had lived a feckless life in New York, sometimes at home, sometimes in the care of the Welfare Department, sometimes just riding the subway round and round at nights. Through tennis she found that her aggression and vitality could actually be useful to her

rather than plunge her into trouble all the time. She grew to welcome the restraints of tennis, which created the perfect setting for her qualities to shine. 'After a while I began to understand that you could walk out on to the court like a lady, all dressed up in immaculate white, be polite to everybody, and still play like a tiger and beat the liver and lights out of the ball. I remember thinking it was kind of like a matador going into the bull ring, beautifully dressed, bowing in all directions, following the fancy rules to the letter, and all the time having nothing in mind except sticking that sword

into the bull's guts and killing him as dead as hell. I probably picked up that notion from some movie I saw.'

Althea, black matador dressed in white. But in the beginning she must have felt as if she were the bull, being goaded and stabbed, and with a mass of people trying to drive her out of the ring. With the help of two southern doctors, Hubert Eaton and Robert Johnson, she had grown to be the best black woman tennis player in the country, winning the championship of the American Tennis Association – the organisation which ran black tennis in the States – ten times in a row as well as studying for a degree at Florida A & M, a black university in Tallahassee.

But being the best black tennis player in the country did not mean she had a chance to play the best white players. The major eastern grass court tournaments were by invitation only – and none were popping through the Gibson letterbox. It was then that Alice Marble, the great pre-war champion, helped change the course of Althea's career. Alice was already something of a heroine to the younger woman, who had once seen her play an exhibition match in New York. Alice, she said, 'impressed me terrifically. Basically, of course, it was the aggressiveness behind her game that I liked. Watching her smack that effortless serve, and then follow it in to the net and put the ball away with an overhead as good as any man's, I saw possibilities in the game of tennis that I had never seen before.'

Alice Marble proceeded with characteristic elegance to put her aggressiveness into action. In *American Lawn Tennis* magazine she set the issue out for her readers. Unless Althea performed well in the eastern tournaments she could not expect to be invited to the National Championships at Forest Hills. Unless she was invited to the eastern tourna-

ments she couldn't play well there. And the Nationals committee were not campaigning vigorously for the tournaments to issue invitations.

'I can't honestly say that I believe Miss Gibson to be a potential champion; I don't know,' she wrote. 'In the Indoors she played under tremendous pressure, but there were moments when she exhibited a bold game that will undoubtedly improve against first class competition. Whether she can achieve championship status here or abroad depends no more on her lovely strokes than on what Althea Gibson finds inside

herself when the chips are down. If she can do it, a proud new chapter will have been added to the history of tennis. If she cannot, we will have seen nothing more and nothing less than one more youngster who failed to live up to her initial promise. But if she is refused a chance to succeed or to fail, then there is an uneradicable mark against a game to which I have devoted most of my life, and I would be bitterly ashamed.'

Her words had as powerful an

Althea Gibson in action. She was as graceful as she was athletic.

Left: **Althea holds up the Wimbledon trophy with only one hand but her grip on it is secure. She won it for the second time in 1958, beating Britain's Angela Mortimer in straight sets.**

Below: **the Queen presenting her with the trophy in 1957 as loser Darlene Hard looks on.**

Opposite: **Althea with Karol Fageros, who was her opponent as a professional. Their matches were the warm-up act for the Harlem Globetrotters. 'The contract called for one hundred matches,' recalls Althea. 'I believe I won about ninety-eight.'**

effect as her tennis had always done, though they were not as universally well received. 'Some of my white so-called friends didn't like what I did,' she recalls today. 'But tough.'

Althea Gibson played the nationals that summer of 1951, winning her first round match out on Court 14 while film star Ginger Rogers played mixed doubles in front of the clubhouse. Althea was unruffled. 'I'd have been pretty backward if I didn't realise that Ginger Rogers was a far greater attraction for the people sitting in the clubhouse porch than Althea Gibson. I would have been far more interested in her myself, and I'm not joking.'

Ginger wasn't a serious contender but then Althea wasn't supposed to be either, and it was a shock to the tennis public when she nearly defeated Louise Brough, the Wimbledon champion. Had a thunderstorm not intervened at 7–6 in the third set for Althea she might well have done so.

The following year she made her first visit to Wimbledon. 'I was awed,' she says now. 'With Wimbledon being such a great establishment I felt very honoured to be invited over to participate my very first time. I felt I was treated decently though I've always wondered all these years as to my very first match, which was against Pat Ward. Why would I be put on Centre Court, someone who's never been there, someone who never had a reputation as a champion tennis player? I wondered if I was put on Centre Court either to show me off or to see me get beaten.'

There was little chance for Wimbledon to do either in the next few years for Althea lost in the second round and was not seen there again till 1956. With her tennis career now secondary to her education it just wasn't possible to raise funds for the trip. It seemed as if the black mata-

dor might be one of the many failures, the ones who end up maimed, scarred or scared. Althea wasn't scared but she was unsure. Not until 1956 did things begin to fall into place. She had been on the verge of giving up tennis when the State Department offered her a trip to Asia.

As a black woman she was an ambassador for a country with an embarrassing public image as far as race relations were concerned. The Supreme Court had ruled in 1954 that American schools should be desegregated and the resulting fury in certain sections of the South had led to a four hundred per cent rise in sales of arms and an incalculable rise in the amount of human misery caused by racial demonstrations, riots and even murders.

Althea was probably chosen for the trip as a public relations exercise. 'At the time I was champion of nothing and unlikely ever to be,' she said. But somewhere in the course of that long tour, some of it enjoyable, some of it a strain, she found the authority of a champion. In 1956 she won the French title and was runner-up at Wimbledon to the indomitable Shirley Fry, in a match said by one writer to have been played in an eerie atmosphere, 'tight-lipped, cold' as the crowd silently willed her white opponent to win.

If that feeling really had been there it was gone by 1957 when Althea, then almost thirty, finally took

the Wimbledon title, beating compatriot Darlene Hard in a fifty minute display so dazzling it might almost have been an exhibition. In 1958 she had another straight sets win, this time over Britain's Angela Mortimer. The following year she turned professional. 'I've read reports about Billie Jean King and other tennis players being the first to make 100,000 dollars as a professional. But I made that then,' she says fiercely, though unlike Billie Jean her money was made, not over the course of a hard fought year of tournaments but for being the opening act on the Harlem Globetrotters' tour and winning approximately ninety-eight of the hundred pro sets she played against Karol Fageros, whose gold lamé panties were more notable than her tennis.

Looked at as a page in the record books her career as a champion was so very short, just three years of major titles, two at Wimbledon, two US Nationals, and one French. But people remember the long-legged, lithe woman with the rangy stride and the tough temperament.

The ironic thing is that they remember her not just as a champion but as the first black champion, something Althea Gibson always resented. She always wanted to be treated as an individual, not as a substitute for the rest of her race. 'At that time I felt I was just representing myself. My people weren't in that sport anyway,' she says now. She's on the move, driven still by restless energy, on the way to sit a civil service exam today, off to Florida for the Superbowl tomorrow and thinking of entering some senior events for next year. But she considers her words carefully. 'I never thought of myself as a spokesman. I was a competitor. I didn't much enjoy being a spokesman for anything.

'But since then I've changed. What I feel right now is that if I played tennis I would be playing for myself and for my people.'

Althea Gibson, former delinquent, is recognised as one of New York's most prominent citizens by the mayor, Robert F. Wagner, as her parents look on. Althea was given a ticker tape reception by the residents of Harlem when she first won Wimbledon in 1957.

9

The Ultimate Centre Court Player

THE CENTRE COURT was empty but not silent. A workman had left his radio on and the slick patter of some Radio One disc jockey tumbled out across the grass, vividly green even in the insipid winter light. The standing room was littered with cardboard and bits of rubble and under that strange sweeping roof the seats were empty. But somehow, as in churches and theatres and all the places which are the setting for scenes of drama and spectacle, there seemed to be a kind of energy trapped here, some latent force that would emerge fully only when the participants and spectators and the atmosphere were right.

The wind whirls and does strange things here. Different things happen to the ball. But it's a great court – you never lose the ball against the background. At Flushing Meadow the ball is constantly in a sea of heads, the same at Kooyong in Australia, but there's no mess around this court, none of the commercial signs that clutter so many centre courts. This is such a pure scene. There is something always very chaste about this court. That is why they have been right to keep the all white dress. It makes Wimbledon special.

The court is just the right size too. You get very close to royalty. It's impossible to calculate how important the presence of royalty is, because it's not tangible, but I would say it has a huge impact.

If ever any player mirrored the image of royalty on court it was Maria Bueno. She was the ultimate Centre Court player, a woman who carried herself like a queen and whose game flourished in this most intense of settings, where every line draws the spectator down to focus on the players on court. Here, where the crowd could look only at her, her always unpredictable tennis became electrifying. She awed spectators with the arrogant grace of her movement, the studied classicism of every shot she hit, her imperious court presence. If Althea Gibson was the matador, brilliant in her suit of lights, Maria was the fine lady accepting the ears of the bull in honour of her beauty.

Her first singles trophy at Wimbledon was in 1959, when she was still only nineteen and one of the youngest champions ever. Despite her youth she came to Wimbledon expecting to win. 'Everybody thought I would at least get to the finals,' she said later. 'I had won the Italian, got to the semis in Paris and lost a match I was expected to win. But I wasn't really planning anything. It just happened. It was a great feeling but I didn't have any sense, "It has to be now."'

She may have had no sense of her own destiny but it was to be a remarkable one. She had a career of great extremes, enduring serious illness which put her out of competition for long periods as well as winning the supreme honours of the game. Her tennis too was one of extremes. 'She was destined to have great wins and great losses right through,' says Lance Tingay. 'She had the most perfect touch and timing but she couldn't afford to go off a little. She hit an absolutely flat ball without any margin of error. Once she was a bit off, the ball was going everywhere and anybody could beat her.'

When she was at her best she could beat anybody, and did, over the years taking three Wimbledon and four US titles. More important

Perfection in action, Maria Bueno had a magnificent all court game, but her serve, right, was her most formidable weapon.

than the number of titles she won, though, was the manner in which she won them. Her tennis was imaginative, artistic, creative, all the things that were missing in the more orthodox tennis of her contemporaries. Play as graceful and inspirational as hers had rarely been seen since the days of Lilli de Alvarez, the flashingly brilliant star of the thirties, who had astonished and delighted Wimbledon audiences not only with her adventurous tennis but also with her spectacular costumes, designed specially for her in Paris.

Maria had Teddy Tinling to design hers, a job he attacked with enthusiasm, giving her a succession of coloured linings beneath her dresses, pale orange, royal purple and finally, to express her hot Latin temperament, shocking pink. This really did shock the Wimbledon authorities, who felt impelled to reiterate their rule on all white dress.

The controversy, trivial though it may have been, helped revive the tournament's flagging fortunes a little. During the late fifties and early sixties, it declined in prestige, mainly because the best men in the world were playing not at Wimbledon but in schools, obscure sports halls and even ice rinks, with boards laid on the ice for the court. As soon as they won Wimbledon they turned professional. Not for the first time, nor the last, the women injected glamour and excitement into the game.

Maria Bueno, with her mixture of fieriness and elegance, was the focus of that excitement, inspiring devoted partisanship from spectators and inflaming the imaginations of a whole generation of schoolgirls. Christine Janes, then, as Christine Truman, the darling of the English crowd, was influenced by her too much, according to Teddy Tinling. 'Had she been able to see Maureen Connolly instead of Maria Bueno as her ideal she might have had a much easier passage to the top,' he said.

Christine was only two years younger than Maria but like many girls of the time, admired the Brazilian so much she wanted to play her attacking game. Even now she still thinks that Maria Bueno on her day was the best she has ever seen. 'She was a very graceful player,' she says wistfully. 'I remember being very

envious of the way she played and thinking I wish I could be like that. I suppose one always wants to be what you're not.'

The rider 'on her day' was essential when talking of Maria Bueno. The fluctuations in her form, sometimes within the course of one match, meant that no opponent was totally without hope against her. 'Maria is a strange player,' commented Britain's Angela Mortimer. 'She is temperamental in the extreme. One day she is brilliant, the next she is brilliantly inaccurate. One day she is smiling and chattering to everyone, the next she is silent and passes her friends without a word.'

As a person she seems to have been something of an enigma, her aloof behaviour incurring the resentment of many of the other players. The women in any case did not have quite the same camaraderie they had had immediately after the war. In the world outside tennis the women of the fifties were being pushed back more and more into their traditional roles of wife and mother. Many were treated as little more than a superior form of interior decoration. Margaret Court coming on to the circuit for the first time, noted dryly that the girls competed as much in their appearance as in their tennis, while gamesmanship went on well into the sixties.

It's much more respectful now. The players used to try and psyche each other out. Some people, if you were due to meet them in the quarter finals, would never talk to you during the week. You can't get away with all that obvious psychological warfare any more because you have to live in each other's pockets so much. There's no cattiness or bitchiness now.

Personal presence probably counted for more then than it does today. Margaret Court talked of being mesmerised by Bueno's 'dark

beauty' and lovely frock as well as the fact that she was Wimbledon champion when they first played. Later that season she overcame that feeling and upset the Brazilian in the quarter finals of the 1960 Australian championships. 'When I finally went into the dressing room Maria was in tears,' she said. 'She didn't speak to me then or at any time before she left Australia. I was shocked that a world champion could behave so badly in defeat. It was a lesson to me, one that would be repeated often in the years to come. I was beginning to realise the enormous pressures on the top player to keep on winning and, more importantly, not to suffer a bad loss. For Maria, the Wimbledon Champion, to lose in the quarter-final round to an unknown junior like myself was a humiliating defeat.'

Maria Bueno had been under pressure before she became world champion. The daughter of a vet in Sao

Left: **Maria Bueno was one of Teddy Tinling's favourite clothes horses, seen left in sixties chic and see-through.**

Below: **Karen Susman, who won Wimbledon in 1963 but gave up competitive tennis to bring up a family. 'Karen was about as good as she ever got by the time she was fifteen or sixteen,' said her doubles partner, Billie Jean King.**

Paolo, she was expected to complete her education as well as carve out a tennis career for herself. The gruelling schedule she kept in 1958 for the month before going abroad allowed her only two hours sleep a night and resulted in a weight loss of seventeen and a half pounds from her slender frame. As she was very attached to her family, particularly her brother Pedro, himself a top Brazilian tennis player, it was hard for her to be away from home for months at a time, as tennis demanded.

And she had the hopes of a nation riding on her. There never had been a South American champion and when Maria won Wimbledon she was showered not only with all the material goods she could have wished for – a car, a house, land – but with the mass adulation of an emotional people. There were ticker-tape welcomes from frenzied crowds; stamps of her were issued; a sixty foot statue of her went up outside the Jockey Club.

But for all the showmanship of her tennis Maria was a very private person who kept her intimate thoughts and feelings to herself and gave her trust to few. The almost hysterical reaction of her fellow countrymen may have taken more out of her emotionally than it gave. Angela Mortimer was on tour in Brazil when Maria celebrated her twenty-first birthday and described the reception she was given. 'Officials surrounded her as she opened their present. She glanced casually at the glittering emerald and diamond necklace and earrings inside the box. Then she shut it again. "Thank you very much," she said quietly, and turned away, completely unmoved or surprised.'

At that time she was undisputed world number one, a title she was not to enjoy again till 1964. Hepatitis intervened, sidelining her for nine months and draining some of her

confidence as well as her strength. Other people stepped in in her absence. Britain's Angela Mortimer winning the title in 1961 and the American Karen Susman, a former pupil of Teach Tennant, winning in 1962. 'She had one chance and she took it with both hands,' says C.M. Jones. 'Just as she and Billie Jean did when they won their first doubles.'

Margaret Smith intervened too and in the next few years they had some of the most exciting battles ever seen in women's tennis, meeting in five finals. Maria won two – the U S in 1963 and Wimbledon in 1964 – while Margaret won three – the French of 1964 and Wimbledon and the Australian in 1965. Both were excitingly aggressive in their method, but they were very differ-

ent in style, Margaret the supreme athlete, Maria the magician, pulling out incredibly difficult shots under pressure and investing the easy ones with such beauty that they looked more impressive than they really were.

She had presence. She had that fantastic body and feline grace on the court and you were left with a fabulous memory. Her tennis presence really came from her heart. It's like when Nureyev stands on the stage. You can't take your eyes off him. It's physical but it's the soul out there as well.

It's strange when you compare her with a player like Martina Navratilova today. With that build and that game and all the rest of it she could dominate women's tennis for the next five years. But she used not to leave me with any memory. You'd watch

Left: **despite appearances to the contrary Maria has just won the 1964 final against Margaret Smith, her great rival.**

Below: **with the losing finalist. This was Bueno's third and final win at Wimbledon. She had beaten the glamorous South African star Sandra Reynolds in the 1959 final, and her doubles partner, American Darlene Hard, in the final of 1960.**

her and say, 'that's amazing', but you wouldn't be left with any emotional feelings. I think Martina's entirely instinctive on the court but I never see a soul out there playing. She's like a Ferrari when everybody else is like any old dreary car. She's got acceleration and you say, wow, 'It's amazing', but I'm not watching a heart and soul out there. It's a phenomenal machine.*

Maria Bueno's talent was the antithesis of mechanical. She may in fact have emphasised the artistic side of her game to the detriment of the whole. 'She was beautiful and feminine and graceful,' says Ann Jones. 'But she was disdainful of anything that was too difficult. She wouldn't play an awkward shot. Say it was too wide or she had to bend to the backhand. If it didn't look nice and wasn't aesthetically attractive, that was it. She wouldn't compromise.'

And the extraordinary thing when you think about their contrasting styles, is that that ethos of the game is most like that of Helen Wills Moody, the great baseliner, who admitted that she never scrambled for balls unless under Mrs Wightman's peremptory orders in their doubles matches. 'To slide, lunge, dive, does not conform to good style in tennis, but there is the dignity of sincerity in the scramble,' she wrote.

Maria Bueno didn't slide, lunge, dive or scramble for balls either. She glided across the court or sprang like a cat, always graceful and fluid and elegant. Had she not been dogged by illness and injury – she eventually had to retire with tennis elbow – she still would probably not have had the staying power to fend off the athleticism and doggedness of Court and King. But nobody showed such a soul as she on the court. Everything she did was flashy, brilliant and beautiful, fitful as fireworks perhaps, but just as satisfying to remember.

The publicity machine rolled right on through the sixties. *Left:* **Ann Jones and Maria Bueno pose on Derry and Toms roof garden for a parade of Teddy Tinling dresses, each one designed to express the personality of its owner.**

Right: 1963 was Margaret Smith's first Wimbledon singles title but Maria Bueno and Darlene Hard were too good for her and her partner, Robyn Ebbern, in the doubles. *Below:* Louise Brough's new partner for the doubles in 1952 was the world's number one, Maureen Connolly. But the two singles finalists of that year could not topple Shirley Fry and Doris Hart.

Below: Althea Gibson, Wimbledon champion in 1957 and 1958, later made her living as a golf professional. *Right:* Maria Bueno, ever graceful, made a brief comeback to singles play in Wimbledon's centenary year, 1977. *Far right:* Margaret Court in 1969, the hard-hitting Australian who won more Grand Slam titles than any other player in history. In 1970, she defeated Billie Jean King in one of the greatest, most competitive finals ever seen at Wimbledon.

Ann Jones fulfilled a lifelong ambition by winning Wimbledon in 1969. She never competed there again.

IO

Grand Slam Greatness

THE WAITING ROOM WAS TINY, too small to contain the emotion of the two women cooped up there together, waiting to play the 1963 Wimbledon singles final. In those few minutes before their match was called, Margaret Smith and Billie Jean Moffitt must have felt as if the waiting had gone on for ever. Rain had washed out their final on Saturday and they had had the whole weekend to wait, to think about the game. Now they were here in this claustrophobic room, as small as a punishment cell in a prison and as cut off from the outside world. The green wall at the end of the Centre Court was only just visible through the frosted glass windows. For both women it was the first Wimbledon final, but it was only the beginning of a decade of waiting in just such small rooms as this, for other finals, in other tournaments as well as Wimbledon.

'It was obvious to almost everyone that unless she fell out of an airplane she was on her way to becoming the next great player in the game. She was tall, powerful, consistent and moved beautifully for a person her size,' said Billie Jean. Later, she herself was to become one of the greatest competitors the game has ever seen, but in 1963 it was Margaret Smith who understood what you need to be a champion. From the age of seventeen, when she had won her first Australian Championship, she had had a sense of purpose. She wanted to be the first Australian woman to win Wimbledon.

Australia had always had its male champions, from Norman Brookes and Gerald Patterson through stylish Jack Crawford to Frank Sedgman, Margaret's own patron as a teenager. Then in the 1950s they came tumbling out one after the other, Hoad, Rosewall, Cooper, Fraser and Laver, as if the country wasn't big enough to hold them all. Margaret Smith was a tennis-mad teenager who wanted to be like them. She wanted to be a champion. Tennis for her was the game they played and it never occurred to her that she might not be able to play it their way. 'I hadn't seen any great women in Australia. And we didn't have television then,' she says. 'But I had seen the men. Also I came from a little country town where I mainly practised with men. They used the serve volley and I just naturally thought that was how you played tennis. Anyway I knew that to get invited to play off the men you *had* to play the way they played.'

The game she brought to Wimbledon in 1963 was hard, fast, athletic and had already won her the US, French, two Italian and three Australian titles. But although her speed and power were dazzling she had a question mark against her temperament. The year before she had become the first top seeded player, man or woman, to go out in the first round of the championship. Her opponent then had been Billie Jean but her own nerves, more than the competitive but still unpolished game of the American girl, had cost her the match.

In 1963, a year later, things were different. Determined to disprove her critics, desperate to fulfil her ambition of taking the title home to Australia, she crunched her way to victory with relentless power, controlling her nerves even when Billie Jean fought back from being 4–0 down in the second set.

Margaret Court became the greatest player of an era that included two truly great players beside herself – Maria Bueno and Billie Jean King. If greatness is to be measured out in Grand Slam titles there has been no one greater. Her total of over sixty, in singles, doubles and mixed, has never been equalled, by man or

woman. But Wimbledon has always been the big one, the world championship of the game. It's the truest test of the champion in tennis, a cauldron bubbling with raw nerves, battered emotions and dramatic situations. To emerge the victor at Wimbledon a player has to be the toughest minded, the bravest of the field. And she has to want the title more than she is afraid of it.

Margaret Court was never happy at Wimbledon, didn't like the crowds, the social atmosphere, 'the whispering, the silence. If someone dropped a penny, you'd hear it fall. American crowds are always busy, very much like those in Australia,' she said. She lost her title to Bueno in 1964, regained it from her the following year and was not to win the singles again at Wimbledon until

Margaret Court was one of the greatest athletes tennis has ever seen.

Margaret with her two great rivals, Billie Jean King, then Little Miss Moffitt, in 1963 (top and centre), and Maria Bueno, whom she beat in 1965.
Billie Jean said of her loss in that 1963 final that it 'stayed with me for a long time. Literally for years afterwards, whenever I needed something to psyche me up before going out to play, I tried to remember the feelings I had during that match, and the sense of utter desolation and failure I felt when we walked off the court. It wasn't a very good feeling and I didn't want to have to repeat it – ever.'

1970, and the greatest match she ever played there. Looking back now she says, 'At Wimbledon I found that nearly every time I was always the number one seed. I always found more pressure on me there. In the early years there was so much expected of me. I don't think I was ready for a lot of it at the time.'

She was the nervous champion, a tall rangy thoroughbred with the long slim limbs and speed of foot of the thoroughbred – and the nervy, finely balanced temperament. Billie Jean was always short and stocky, a lively little working horse of a girl with a big heart and a great capacity for hard graft. For all her on-court eccentricity, the excited chatter and public conversations with herself, she probably had the stronger match temperament of the two, winning Wimbledon twice as often as the Australian, even though Margaret Court dominated many of those years. 'She's the the greatest player I've ever met,' said Ann Jones of Court. 'But not the greatest match player. On the very important occasions she can tighten up.'

Astonishingly for a woman with such great gifts, the reason was her basic insecurity.

She was definitely insecure and she got very nervous playing. I was her doubles partner at various points through her career. Together we won three US doubles titles, the French and the Australian, both in 1973. A couple of the Australians nearly had nervous breakdowns playing with her! But I understood her well enough not to worry. She could be a bit brutal to play doubles with although she was so fantastically good. If she was having a bad day and hadn't been playing well, maybe missing a whole lot of balls, and then suddenly I'd miss one, I would be the one to blame. But that was because she was insecure. We played well together because I understood my role. She was a way better

player than I was. I would just set the ball up and she would put it away. She was tremendous.

But in singles she was vulnerable to people being very tough psychologically and they could get through to her. You had a feeling that she had a bit of a battle with herself because she was very aware of those things and frightened by them. In order to overcome them she had to make herself a

little aloof. I think some of the players resented that.

They may also have resented her sheer physical strength, the crushing power of a game that seemed to have no weaknesses. For all the nervousness that beset her at Wimbledon Margaret was a gritty competitor, who never gave up and had the champion's gift of playing her best shots in her worst crises.

I watched so many of her matches, or played in them, when there would be a crisis point. If she survived it she'd be sailing for the rest of the match. She put all her money into this one vital point with the assurance of someone flipping a two-headed coin.

As a champion in full flow she was simply thrilling, a ruthless aggressor who crunched the ball away. Bueno was all grace and touch, Billie Jean a constant experimenter with the ball. Court destroyed the ball. She was faster and bigger and stronger than any other woman, and must have been an awe-inspiring sight on the other side of the net. She had built her body up through gruelling sessions in the gym, training with male athletes and footballers. 'She would always hold her own,' said Stan Nichols, her trainer. 'Some of them dodged her, because they didn't want to be shown up by a woman.' In one set of fitness tests she finished third against a group of men, with only Frank Sedgman and one of Australia's top Olympic athletes ahead of her.

Many people spoke of her as being a manufactured player who'd got where she had through hard work, and she was one of the most dedicated workers the game has known, almost austere in her approach to training. A devout Catholic, she once said she thought nuns and priests should continue to sacrifice their private lives to God; this at a time when progressive elements within the church were calling for a relaxation of the law on priestly chastity. But Margaret Court understood that kind of sacrifice, gave her life to tennis with that kind of commitment.

Only when she retired for a while, at the age of twenty-four, did she make time in her life for romance, returning to the circuit in 1968 with a husband, Barry Court, to accompany her.

Opposite: **Margaret Court's serve had a punishing force. She was one of the strongest women ever to grace the court. In 1973 her strength and her luck ran out. Her face shows the anguish of defeat to the American teenage star Chris Evert in the Wimbledon semi-finals.**

She was more than just a hard worker, though, and had great natural gifts that she developed to the utmost. She had a reach three inches longer than the average woman, a hand strength as great as that of many male athletes. And although Billie Jean said she had 'bad hands,' she was one of the most incisive volleyers ever in women's tennis. 'To me it was exciting,' says Margaret. 'I loved to volley. It was natural to me as I started very young. To come in and put away a high backhand volley, that's the exciting part.'

Perhaps the volley, so satisfying to crunch away out of reach of an opponent, fulfilled a basic ruthlessness in her. Right from a very early age she was stubborn. After the first trip abroad in 1961 she refused to travel again with Mrs Nell Hopman, a former player and wife of Harry, the Australian Davis Cup coach. She said simply they did not 'get on', though she also felt that Mrs Hopman's desire to bring the tour home under budget meant the players' needs as athletes were secondary to economic considerations. What shocked her most was that several officials whose support she sought refused to give it for political reasons. This experience made her dislike tennis administrators and she steadfastly refused ever again to get mixed up in tennis politics. In later years this led to charges of selfishness when she would not join the original Virginia Slims tour, but she was unrepentant. As a married woman she did not want to sign up for sixteen events as the Slims rules required. So she just didn't.

That dogged quality, popularly known as downright bloody-mindedness, took her to victory in her greatest ever match at Wimbledon, the 1970 final against the woman who had always been her toughest rival, Billie Jean King. The match was the longest final in the women's history, forty-six brutal games played over two hours twenty-seven minutes, just sixteen minutes less than the five set final played by John Newcombe and Ken Rosewall that year.

Newcombe and Rosewall were two of the great players in the men's game, but their final is not remembered with the awe which surrounds the women's final. It was hard fought but if the truth were told, the two were not evenly matched. Newcombe was in his prime, Rosewall more than a little past his. Margaret Court and Billie Jean King had been rivals for almost a decade, with first one, then the other gaining the ascendancy. Now for the first time they were going in to a Wimbledon final with equal status. In the eyes of most of those who watched it, this match was the showdown, the crunch match, the one that would settle once and for all just who was the greater.

In later years Billie Jean was to denigrate the match. Margaret's ankle was so badly injured she had it shot full of novocaine just before they came on. Billie Jean's knee was so bad she had to have an operation on it the following week. The press, said Billie Jean, had confused competition with quality. 'Oh yeah,' she wrote, 'if either one of us had played up to our average form, the other would have been lucky to take a couple of games.'

But tennis is more than just strokes and strategy. Sport goes beyond the physical. The 1970 final was passionate, raw, almost primitive in its pitting of indomitable will against indomitable will. Court and King were like two heavyweights of the game that day, bludgeoning each other with all the power, the attacking spirit, the sheer guts they had at their disposal. If Court had had nerves before, she lost them now, clawing back a deficit in both sets when Billie Jean took the lead. She fought every point of the way, and she had to, because Billie Jean did too. In the end she won by the narrowest of margins, 14–12, and 11–9, perhaps the greatest win of her career, as great an achievement in itself as the Grand Slam that she finally sealed later that year by winning the U S Open.

And in a way that great match, the supposed showdown, the crunch, didn't solve anything at all. The

Margaret Court with her son Danny. She was one of the few women to combine motherhood with the life of a touring pro.

spirit in which it was played transcended the result. All her career Margaret Court had fought the nerves inside her as well as the great competitor on the other side of the net that day. Now she had beaten both, she was again Wimbledon champion, she had won. But Billie Jean King hadn't lost.

II

Going for the Big One

SHE DIDN'T HAVE THE POWER and athleticism of Margaret Court and she wasn't as graceful as Maria Bueno. She was small for an attacking player, only five foot four, and she had dodgy knees and she never weighed the same thing twice. She was excitable, always talking to herself on court – she never felt the same thing twice either. But when you got down to basics, if you were actually going to put *money* on it, you would have to go for Billie Jean.

An American columnist once said of Billie Jean King that she had never forgiven Nature for the dirty trick it played on her, preventing her playing for the Green Bay Packers.

But had Billie Jean been born a man she would have been best suited, not for a team game like American football, but for the one to one combat sports, where you get a showdown

The formidable American Wightman cup team of 1962. From left, Karen Susman, Margaret Varner, Margaret Osborne DuPont (playing captain), Darlene Hard, Billie Jean Moffitt, and Nancy Richey.

at the end and it's just two people facing each other and all the money and all the prestige in the world depend on it. She would have been the greatest heavyweight champion the world has seen.

That first match which shot her to prominence – the one when she shocked Margaret Smith at Wimbledon – gave people the wrong image of her. As little Miss Moffitt she seemed cute, engaging, lively, a funny little oddball who charmed

Wimbledon audiences without ever disturbing their conviction that her win had been a fluke and she wasn't really a threat to the top names in the game, the Buenos and Smiths and Hards.

But Billie Jean King was more dangerous than that. She had always had an inner certainty, untarnished by any experience to the contrary, that she would one day be the best in the world.

As a child she was the original tomboy, thrilled when her father made her her own baseball bat and played with her in the yard. But baseball was for boys – still is, for that matter. Tennis was the one game which allowed her to run and jump and thump out at a ball without being considered unladylike. The daughter of a fireman in Long Beach, California, she was entering a prosperous middle class sport where her homemade shorts and lavender coloured nylon-strung racquets marked her out from the other youngsters. Her family were not poor, just less prosperously middle class than those around them, but that relative lack of wealth drove Billie Jean on to succeed.

It 'gave me a great drive', she wrote. 'I read somewhere that Jack Nicklaus's family belonged to a country club when he was growing up, but his father was a druggist, and in the country club pecking order that wasn't much, so it drove Nicklaus to work harder to excel at golf than the other, relatively more privileged, boys did. Maybe that's the best of all worlds you could have when growing up – poorest kid in the country club.' In that drive to succeed, tennis became more than a game to Billie Jean.

I always assumed that her moti-

Billie Jean King won her first Wimbledon singles title in 1966, defeating Maria Bueno in the final.

*vation came from the fact that win-
ning made her really somebody. Winning gave her power. I remember her
once even saying, 'If I make money
then nobody can look down at me.'*

When Billie Jean came into tennis
it was still an amateur game, with
cash payments of 'expenses' being
given out by officials in the Wimbledon Tea Room tucked into little
white envelopes. The fact that the
men's champion could receive as
much as five times what she did in-
furiated Billie Jean, as did the fact
that the little white envelope system
even existed. 'It was the hypocrisy
of the thing that bugged me most,'
she said. 'I wanted the chance to
make money, honest money, doing
what I did best. It was that simple.'

She got going as the sixties started
swinging; has always somehow expressed the mood of the times – the
graph of her personal life swooping
up and down through open marriage, women's liberation, open tennis, abortion and bisexuality as these
subjects were being discussed in
public. She had her twentieth birthday on the day John F. Kennedy was
shot down in Dallas, a day when the
West suddenly seemed to lose its self
assurance. But if the world has
seemed a messier, harder, more restless place since then, Billie Jean has
always known that there was no
safety within the white lines of the
tennis court. No hiding place.

In 1964 she committed herself,
after four seasons of treating tennis
as little more than her summer hol-
iday, to channelling all of her un-
doubted energy into the game. She
was offered a winter's training in
Australia with Mervyn Rose, a
former player who had become one
of the finest coaches in the world.
She went, admitting she was 'shoot-
ing to be number one'. 'It scared me
to put myself on the line like that
but I understood that if I declared
my honest intentions in the open, it

Billie Jean and Margaret before
their epic final in 1970. Neither
was fully fit, but the match was
unforgettable.

Defeat for Billie Jean in the memorable final of 1970, left. But the taste of victory again in 1972 against Evonne Goolagong (*opposite*).

would drive me all the more,' she said. She allowed Rose to take her game apart and put it all back together again with a new forehand and a slice serve instead of the American twist she had favoured before.

The result was temporary failure, but the following season she reached the final of the 1965 US Open, losing yet again to Margaret Smith. In 1966, five years after she and Karen Hantze had giggled their way to the Wimbledon doubles title, she finally won her first Wimbledon singles title. She started off her career as a champion as she was always to conduct it, by winning the big one. Billie Jean liked to play off emotion, any emotion, and if there was none there she would psyche herself up till she had manufactured it. At Wimbledon she didn't often have to do that. The desire for the big one, the respect for it, was always there driving her on.

Her opponent in the 1966 final was Maria Bueno, whose long, dancer's legs and dancer's grace made her the most charismatic woman in the game. Billie Jean, by contrast, was short and stocky, having to compensate for her lack of long dancer's legs with an almost acrobatic athleticism, and keeping the ball away from Maria's long dancer's arms by using perhaps her greatest weapon, a shrewd tactical brain.

Billie Jean has always been noted for resisting the things she found unfair, and Maria's reputation just happened to be one of them. 'As far as tennis was concerned I never thought she knew what was going on out there,' said Billie Jean. 'She was a con, really, because it would have been blasphemy for anybody ever to

suggest that someone who looked that good could be lacking.' But she had one of the things Billie Jean always wanted – the crowd's affection. Her own strengths were too cerebral, her determination to win too relentless to be endearing, and if the Wimbledon crowds had found her mannerisms amusing at first, they began, after a while, to be embarrassed by them.

One of the problems for Billie Jean was that the other two champions of the day, Margaret Court and Maria Bueno, made the things they were good at look easy. Billie Jean had neither their reach nor their height. Her success was obviously hard won, fashioned as much out of effort and will-power as out of her more facile gifts of speed and natural co-ordination.

Billie Jean King and Chris Evert after the 1973 final, won by the older woman. Despite the generation gap the two champions understood each other.

Opposite: **Evonne Goolagong Cawley took her second Wimbledon title in 1980, much to the delight of herself, her family – and the Centre Court crowds, who adored her.**

Rain soaks the Centre Court in 1980, an unfortunate occurrence, but not unique!

Below: Billie Jean King's devastating backhand was still not enough to win her the 1970 final. In 1983 *(opposite)*, nearly forty, she was beaten by eighteen-year-old Andrea Jaeger in the semi-finals.
Left: Billy Jean wins her sixth Wimbledon singles title in 1975.

Britain's Virginia
Wade in that
fairytale final in
1977. She threw
her arms in the air
– 'Our Ginny' had
won Wimbledon –
and in the Queen's
Jubilee Year too.

She was very powerful. She always has been. From way back. When I played against her the major thing I had to do was forget she was Billie Jean. Like most great players she imposed her personality on you. She had a terribly powerful personality out there. I don't think spectators identified with her very much. They were sort of puzzled by her, but fascinated. They do watch her on the court but I am never sure that they feel comfortable. They look at her as almost an exception.

Where Maria Bueno was a soul on court, Billie Jean was an ego. She introduced a tough professionalism into the glory business of winning the greatest amateur tennis championship in the world. In three years during the sixties she took the title away from crowd favourites – Bueno in 1966, Britain's Ann Jones in 1967, and one of the jolliest underdogs ever to be cheered on by the Centre Court crowd, Australian Judy Tegart in 1968. The unbroken run of victories ended in 1969, the year two American astronauts took the first walk on the moon. Billie Jean couldn't reach this superhuman level of achievement and went down in three sets to a newly aggressive Ann Jones.

But the year before, as well as achieving her third successive title, she had done what she had always wanted to do. By winning in 1968 Billie Jean King was able to take home a pay cheque from Wimbledon and not a £30 voucher for Harrods. The All England Club had been pressing for tennis to go open from as far back as 1959. Finally, in December 1967 Britain's Lawn Tennis Association, responding from pressure from the All England Club, had voted to abolish the distinction between amateurs and professionals. The ruling was to take effect from April 22, 1968, the first day of the English Hard Court

Championships in Bournemouth. This unilateral decision forced an agreement from the International Lawn Tennis Federation that every country could make its own decisions regarding amateurism and professionalism.

The tennis world had been created anew, except for one thing. Adam was still taking home twice as much as Eve – Billie Jean won £750 in 1968, while Rod Laver won £2000. The world was not brave enough or new enough for Billie Jean King and in the seventies she found herself acting as spokeswoman for 'Women's Lob', as the movement for equal pay in tennis was quickly nicknamed. When the Pacific Southwest Open in Los Angeles offered a prize money ratio of twelve to one in 1970, Billie Jean and a group of women pros decided to stage an alternative tournament. Gladys Heldman, publisher of *World Tennis* magazine, staged it for them and helped find the women the sponsorship that was to enable them to break completely from the men. 'You've Come a Long Way, Baby,' was the advertising slogan of the Virginia Slims tobacco company and the Slims circuit took the women almost all the way.

But there were bitter struggles before they won their professional autonomy. The Slims women had defied the US Lawn Tennis Association by refusing to pay it a share of their gate receipts. In 1971 the Association refused to sanction the Slims and instead set up its own rival circuit, threatening to have the women banned from the major international championships. The new stars, Evonne Goolagong and Chris Evert, afraid of missing the Grand Slam events, elected to compete on the official USLTA tour. Billie Jean had the most arduous and the most satisfying role of her career. She was champion of a cause, strid-

Billie Jean's great doubles partnership with the spectacular Rosie Casals (*above*) took her four titles further along the road to her record twenty titles. *Right:* Billie Jean crashed to an unexpected defeat against the Russian Olga Morozova, seeded eighth, in the 1974 quarter-final.

ing out in every match with something to fight for. She was, at last, the underdog, taking on the might of the official association. An ego on the court perhaps, but one harnessed in the service of an ideal.

She had been beaten by Evonne Goolagong in the 1971 Wimbledon semi-finals. In the US Open semis that year she faced an even more dangerous opponent, Chris Evert. At sixteen, Chris was the sensation of the Open, having beaten three established players, Mary Ann Eisel, Françoise Durr and Lesley Hunt to get to the semis. 'A monster had been created and I had to put an end to it,' said Billie Jean. Had Chris beaten the top draw on the Slims tour and, even worse, gone on to win the Open, her victory would, Billie Jean felt, destroy the Slims tour and with it women's professional tennis.

Billie Jean had based her whole career on a rock solid fear of losing. 'The best players, I think, are always the ones who remember their losses because they remember the pain and they hate it,' she said, describing seeing Rod Laver after he had been upset in the fourth round of the 1970 Wimbledon by Roger Taylor. 'I'll never forget the look on his face. It was as though someone had ripped the guts from his belly.' Now she was playing with fire in her belly, afraid to lose, not just for herself but for all the women who had fought for their professional integrity.

That fire and fear carried her to a straight sets win over Chris. Later they were to become close friends. The aggressive net-rusher and the cool baseliner had much in common. 'Sometimes, I can't completely dissociate myself – not when Chris is playing, anyway,' said Billie Jean later. 'I'll never feel for any of the others the way I do for her. It'll always seem a little more painful when she loses, because she became some part of me on the court, and no mat-

In 1973 Billie Jean was attempting to create the Women's Tennis Association. That was the year of the men's Wimbledon boycott and she went to their union, the Association of Tennis Professionals, and offered the women's support. 'Get the picture: the men have a dispute, and we are offering, free and clear, no strings attached, to stick our necks out and support them,' she wrote. 'They wouldn't even respond.' And with a full women's draw and a new star in Bjorn Borg Wimbledon survived.

Agony and determination from Billie Jean, always the perfectionist. 'I was very intense about everything I did,' she said. 'If I didn't win a point just exactly the way I wanted to, if the ball didn't skim the net and land two inches from the line I'd get really upset. And off the court I was the same way. I'd bowled maybe twenty-five times in my entire life, yet every time I went up to that line I expected to knock all the pins down.'

ter who won, each of us needed the other, because you're more of a player, not just for winning, but for beating someone special. And we always understood that, both of us.'

Ironically the most special person Billie Jean King ever beat was not a woman at all, but Bobby Riggs, the 1939 Wimbledon men's champion, a man who even in his prime was seen as a less attacking player than Alice Marble, the ladies champion for that year. Riggs had beaten Mar-

garet Court in the first of his male-female challenge matches, but then Margaret had never had a fire in her belly for women's tennis. She had only ever wanted to be a champion. There was no title going in that Mother's Day match and Court's ladylike spirit quailed and competitive spirit failed when faced with the Riggs ballyhoo. 'That kind of crack-up happens to everybody one or two times in his or her career and it's just unfortunate that it hit her on that particular day,' said Billie Jean. 'I felt sorry for her and I think there must have been great sympathy for her from everybody who watched the match.'

Court v Riggs was just the warm-up match, though. The Billie Jean match was the one Bobby, a self confessed hustler, had wanted all along. In competitive terms it was meaningless. Billie Jean, at almost thirty, was in her prime, while Bobby, his stomach rattling around with almost as many vitamin pills as Barbara Cartland's, was fifty-five and not. There had even been many more significant male-female contests in the past. Suzanne Lenglen and Pauline Betz had both played exhibitions against the leading male players of their day, Suzanne against Bill Tilden and Pauline against Jack Kramer, while Mrs Hazel Wightman had even made a habit of it. Around 1908 she had gone on trips to the North West and often been asked to play against men. In those days the battle of the sexes was not as bitter as in the 1970s and Mrs

Wightman usually won, mainly because the custom was for the man to start playing his best only after the woman had built up a big lead.

Suzanne and Pauline were both annihilated by their opponents and there is no doubt that had Billie Jean been facing Stan Smith or Jimmy Connors she would have been badly beaten too. At this level the men are going to cover the court quicker and they're more powerful. Even a player as powerful as Martina would probably only get a couple of games from the top men.

But Bobby Riggs was not a top man. And he hadn't played for $100,000 before. Nor was he playing on behalf of his half of the human race. To Bobby it was simply the greatest hustle he had organised in his whole career. But to Billie Jean it was a crusade. If she lost this one she felt she would let down the whole of women's tennis. The pressure was perhaps the greatest of her whole career, but then Billie Jean had always played her best tennis under pressure. Strong emotion had to be there for her to be really en-

gaged in the outcome of her own matches.

She could not have invented a more appropriate showcase for her own extrovert talents. The audience was the largest ever in the history of tennis, 30,492 people packed into Houston's Astrodome to watch Billie Jean being carried in on a litter in her rhinestone-studded Teddy Tinling dress. The male chauvinist piglet that was presented to Bobby

Billie Jean's triumphal entry to the Astrodome where she beat Bobby Riggs (*below*) **in straight sets.**

Riggs went squealing off to hide in a dark corner of the Astrodome, overwhelmed by the noise and the spectacle of the occasion.

Billie Jean loved it. Off court she is the great adventurer of the game, pressing ahead to new goals, inspired always by the future rather than the present. On court she has often been less adventurous than she wanted to be, eschewing the spins she loves, the crazy, flashy shots that get an audience going, in favour of a shrewder, more percentage type of tennis. 'It kills me to admit it, but I'm a duller player because of my need to win,' she has said. That day, against Riggs, she was dazzling, out-thinking the man who had the shrewdest tactical brain in the game, wrong-footing him, manoeuvring him all over the court, destroying him with a fireworks display of brilliant backhands from all over the court. During the whole of the three set match, The Big One, the pressure match of all time, she had hit sixty-four per cent outright winners – shots totally out of Riggs' reach.

And even the three Wimbledons, the three US Opens and the French title she won during the seventies, the record twenty titles at Wimbledon, may not have meant as much to her or been as crucial for women's tennis as that brilliant farcical match against Bobby Riggs.

She's still here, still around at forty, really the Old Lady now amongst all the high school kids, though she's been calling herself that for a decade now. She's the age Mrs Lambert Chambers was when she played Suzanne Lenglen in their historic final of 1919, but who, in these most competitive of times, would have expected her to reach the Wimbledon semi-finals in 1982 and 1983 and throw in the 1983 mixed doubles final as well?

Margaret Court, her great rival, never appeared to be able to bring herself to like her but 'I admire her,' she says. 'For her to be still playing the way she plays today, to get to the semis of Wimbledon at forty, that shows how good she used to be.'

There's a scene in Billie Jean's favourite film, *Chariots of Fire*, where runner Harold Abrahams tells his girlfriend, 'I won't run if I can't win.' She is scathing. 'If you don't run you can't win,' she says, telling him not to come back to her until he's sorted that one out.

It's an equation Billie Jean King has never had any problem with.

The last poignant look at the Centre Court. Defeat for Billie Jean in the 1983 semi-finals to teenager Andrea Jaeger. 'I've never looked over my shoulder before, but I took a last look around at the end, just in case I didn't come back,' she said later.

Opposite: **Christine Truman won this three set Centre Court thriller in 1961 against that year's Australian champion, Margaret Smith.**

12

Great Expectations

IT'S A CLASSIC MOMENT, the moment of winning Wimbledon, one that only three British players since the war have experienced. The ritual is always the same, the red carpet rolled out, the handshake with royalty, the thrusting of the trophy high in the air. But the feeling is different for everyone. Virginia Wade wanted to run around and hug everybody on the Centre Court; sensible, practical Ann Jones had to take a drink to stop herself from crying; Angela Mortimer knew she had played 'pretty appalling stuff' that day. But she didn't care. Holding the trophy high above her head, she wanted to retire right there and then.

For all three of these British champions that moment of victory was more than just a moment. It was the culmination of years of work, years of hope, years of desire. Not one of them won Wimbledon casually or easily and their success when it did come was sweeter, brought more lasting emotion.

It's always been harder for the Brits at Wimbledon than anybody else. No matter how highly Wimbledon is valued by players from all over the world as the greatest championship in the game, it means just that bit more to the British. It's their tournament, with too many people wanting them to win, too many to criticise them when they fail.

Many of the top British players have played their worst tennis at Wimbledon, perhaps none more so than Virginia Wade herself. Always spectacular, whether in the right way or the wrong way, she was too tense to relax there, too intense to be philosophical about her chances. 'She has been pitiable to watch,' wrote Rex Bellamy of *The Times*. 'Her highly strung nerves jumping around as if an imaginary dentist was going berserk with the drill.'

Much of the reason is the pressure put on players by the British press. Margaret Court, who suffered from the opposite situation in her own country and once said she felt like an anonymous champion there, considered that the British press 'kill their own players. They always expect so much of them, almost pleading with them to win. Then they rubbish them when they lose. Virginia Wade never can play her best at Wimbledon because she knows so much is expected of her, particularly from the press.'

The interesting thing is that this dead weight of other people's expectations, which can kill a player's enterprise and spontaneity, is being felt now by young players all over

the world and not just in Britain – from parents, national federations, coaches, agents, managers. 'It's one of the tragedies of the game at the moment, not only in the women's game but also in the men's,' says Virginia. 'They get so much money and attention now. I did, when I was seventeen, and I was put on a pedestal far too soon. In fact what happened in Britain with British tennis players is now happening worldwide. The British were always so desperate to have a good tennis player that they would see you were promising and say how wonderful you were and that you were the one great hope and all the rest of it. Of course they raise you up before you really should be there, so the moment you don't come through with the goods then they start throwing stones and pulling you down.

'Now it's happening worldwide. The media are desperate for stories about anybody who looks good. America especially is guilty of this. The first thing anybody ever asks me is, "Who are the best of the youngsters? Who do you see that is coming along?" And then they latch on to those names.'

In Britain the pressure is compounded by the fact that attention is focussed so entirely on one person. 'There are not too many British hopes,' says Angela Mortimer wryly. 'There were always more Americans. They had much more depth. You'd only have a couple at the top here, whereas they could go right down to about ten. If one was off colour there was always someone else. It makes you try too hard sometimes.'

Both she and Christine Truman, her opponent in the 1961 final, were tryers by nature. They had both won the French championship, the title which is tailor-made for the breed, Christine doing so at eighteen years

True Brits. *Left:* **Angela Mortimer, who won the 1961 Wimbledon final against the darling of the Centre Court, Christine Truman,** *right.*

five months, still the youngest ever winner. Angela's tennis career had only got off the ground in the first place because she was a tryer, pestering coach Arthur Roberts (who later brought Sue Barker to prominence) until he took her on. Her greatest natural talent was her ability to work hard. She built herself an all-court game, stroke by stroke, though she was a rock steady baseliner by choice and temperament. At twenty-nine she was still playing in spite of the deafness that had been diagnosed when she was twenty-two, in spite too of the entamoebic dysentery she had had in 1956 after a tour of Egypt and which had caused her weight to drop from nine stone to just six and a half.

Although her determination and patience were much admired, it was Christine Truman who was actually given the affection of the Wimbledon crowd. A large raw-boned girl with a jolly, English face and a jolly English disposition, she was loved for the uninhibited way she played, her patent love of thumping that great big forehand of hers, and also for the generous way she lost. Angela Mortimer was aware of the crowd's preference though she reckoned the hardest thing was playing someone you knew you should beat. 'Someone like Christine could hit a blind spot and turn the records upside down,' she says.

Christine took the first set of the final 6–4 and then after a forty minute break for rain – only too appropriate for this first all-British final since 1914 – was a point away from a 5–3 lead in the second. Turning to reach a lob from Angela she fell heavily. The older woman caught up

and passed her in that set, then took a hard fought third set at 7–5.

No match, of course, is won or lost on one point, though some players appear to think so. Christine's game *did* fizzle out after that moment, but then Angela was a determined fighter, never more dangerous than when she was behind. She had won matches from more hopeless positions than this. Bea Seal, one time Wightman Cup captain, says that Christine had injured her ankle the winter before in the West Indies and had been diagnosed as having a thrombosis. 'I think Christine got frightened about this thrombosis

business. Angela Mortimer was too brainy for her after that and lobbed everything over her head or drop-shotted her. Angela played the game rather like a game of chess, I always thought.'

Her ability to manipulate the game by brain-power rather than physical power was one she shared with Ann Jones, the 1969 champion. Ann has the lean, strong-jawed face and down-to-earth look of the pioneer women. You can imagine her in a faded print dress, riding the waggon-train with a baby in one arm and a shotgun in the other. She is one of the most tenacious women who has ever played the game of tennis, clear-eyed about her own talents, modest in her aims. 'She had a lot of guts and was unbelievably hard to play against,' said Billie Jean

King. 'I'd say Ann wore me out more often than any other player I've ever faced.'

Her critics condemned her for being cautious and boring, though Virginia, her team-mate on so many Wightman Cup sides, disagrees. 'Boring tennis and being tenacious and hanging on is different. On clay especially Ann never gave a point away. She played a fairly defensive game but she wasn't boring. She was a very very intelligent tennis player.'

Her caution was only partly the result of her own nature. A great competitor she once said she would stay on the baseline three hours if she knew she would win. But she was lacking in self belief. She believed the critics who said she had got where she had only through hard work. She 'impressed us with her

capacity to push her talent to, and apparently beyond its logical limit,' wrote Rex Bellamy of *The Times*.

But it wasn't entirely fair. As a youngster her main sport had been table tennis, in which she was runner-up in the world championships in 1957. Table tennis, even more than tennis, requires two natural skills, speed of reflex and superb hand-eye co-ordination. That Ann Jones excelled in the sport indicates what natural gifts she had as a ball player.

Her breakthrough at Wimbledon after seven semi-finals and one final came after she had acted like the pioneer she resembled and joined three other women – Billie Jean King, Rosie Casals and Françoise Durr – in George McCall's professional troupe in 1968. That gave her

Angela Mortimer (*left*) **and Christine Truman** (*above*). **The British more than anyone were under pressure at Wimbledon.**

Ann Jones brought the sixties to a close with a bang. She beat Billie Jean King in three sets in the 1969 final.

players in the history of women's tennis – Margaret Court in the semis and Billie Jean King in the final – playing tennis as aggressive as theirs. This new departure for her was the last great flourish of her career. Had she learned to play the attacking game earlier that career might have been even more successful than it was.

Aggression is a quality that never eluded Virginia Wade. Underneath the gracious off-court exterior of extremely well brought up, well educated, intelligent and rational arch-deacon's daughter was a turbulence, an explosiveness that was as inexplicable as it was unpredictable. Writers often use the word 'volcanic' to describe a tempestuous nature. In Virginia's case it was

particularly apt; the smooth innocuous looking surface but beneath it, a boiling mass of energy liable to erupt at any time.

That energy gave Virginia Wade a court persona unlike anyone else's. Angela Mortimer, Christine Truman and Ann Jones were all terribly British, the kind of intrepid women who would have been the backbone of the Empire. Virginia, for all her chipped upper middle class voice, her classic English elegance, appeared strangely un-British, a wild, exotic, passionate creature who was regarded with proprietorial pride but also some perplexity. Teddy Tinling once said his dresses for her expressed the fact that she wanted to appear part of the Establishment but was really a tigress un-

the opportunity to practise consistently with some of the greatest men in the world, an experience she looks back on with gratitude.

'The tennis world is narrow and you're very much on your own. We didn't have the benefit of practice and training the players get these days. It wasn't very easy in Birmingham, where I come from. One was making do rather than doing something more positive. When we played with the Stolles and Emersons and Lavers we all benefited but I think I did more than the others. It was an opening of the mind to what I'd got to do. Had I realised earlier that I was capable of playing that aggressive tennis I might have won Wimbledon sooner. They convinced me that I could do it before I would do it physically. It was the way they practised, and they loved the game so much. They really would play with anybody. They'd hit with kids in the park.'

She took that new self belief and aggression to Wimbledon in 1969 and beat two of the most aggressive

Teddy Tinling with the top stars. Virginia Wade, Evonne Goolagong, Rosie Casals and Billie Jean King model his original 'Dacron' creations in 1973.

Below: **Virginia reached the last sixteen that year, only to be defeated by Evonne Goolagong 6-3 6-3 on the Centre Court.**

derneath. British audiences, unused to such emotional extravagance, probably saw the tigress first.

It was what made her a star. Like her heroine, Maria Bueno, she had an imperiousness, a hauteur that drew the eye to her. With that big penetrating serve timed as faster than many men's, her bold volleying, her fierce athleticism, she made every tennis match a drama. A soul on the court. But unlike Bueno's, her soul's primary urge was not an aesthetic one. Where Bueno's game was an invitation to the spectator to look at her, see how beautiful it all was, Wade's was a furious command to look at her, see how exciting and spectacular it all was.

The passion she invested in her tennis was overt. When things went wrong it could spill over into scenes, breaking the bounds of normal court

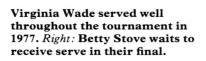

Virginia Wade served well throughout the tournament in 1977. *Right:* Betty Stove waits to receive serve in their final.

Opposite: **In 1983 Virginia, competing for the twenty-second time, reached the quarter-finals, and was the last surviving British player in the singles championship.**
Below: **The spotlight focusses on Virginia after the Queen has presented the trophy to her in 1977.**

etiquette. But if Virginia was unlike her more stoic compatriots in this, she shared one very important quality with them. Billie Jean King, not always complimentary about her, said, 'Never say that Virginia Wade didn't have guts and didn't try ... Virginia had a fine serve and forehand but she couldn't hit anything down the line. I fed her junk all the time. But it didn't matter what the score was: she'd never pack it in, never stop going for it.'

But it took Virginia Wade the better part of her career to learn to use the qualities within her to their utmost. Now that tennis had become a big money sport there were more opportunities for self-improvement than there had ever been. Virginia enlisted the help of the late Jerry Teeguarden in her Wimbledon year. 'Technically I was potentially very good but I don't think that I was ever quite as good as I could have been because I needed to correct things. For that you need to have a very good coach all the way along,' she says.

More than the physical faults, though, she learned to correct the mental weaknesses that had barred her way to the very top of the game. The curious thing was that off court Virginia was one of the most cerebral of the women, highly intelligent and cultured. On court she sometimes seemed to have forgotten to bring her brain with her – her love of the spectacular would always triumph over her need to win. Now for the first time she was dispassionate about what she needed to do, and passionate about doing it. She had never committed herself totally to the sport before, despite her total commitment when actually on the court.

'People kept asking me afterwards if I had changed after I won Wimbledon or if winning Wimbledon changed my life. Really it was

because I had managed to change my life that I won. I was so sure I was going to win I put everything into that and I didn't have any emptiness then when I did it. I did when I won the US Open in 1968. I didn't know how I had done it or how I was going to repeat it. When that happens you're afraid to win because you don't want to have to come out and be expected to do it the next day.'

The next day after Wimbledon 1977 was reserved for a champagne celebration. Virginia Wade had beaten Chris Evert, the world's number one woman, in the semifinal, and then Holland's Betty Stove in the euphoric final played out in front of the Queen. It was centenary year for Wimbledon. Jubilee Year for one Queen and Jubilee Day for another, and one of the most emotional scenes the Centre Court has ever witnessed.

But then arousing people's emotion, more even than playing wild, bold, exciting tennis, is what Virginia Wade does best. 'You either wanted Virginia to win or you wanted her to lose,' says Bea Seal. 'But you always wanted something.'

The hand that says it all, 'the ball was *out*!'

13

Evonne Goolagong, stretching for a wide ball. She loved to run. 'I like a good perspire,' she said once.

Walkabout at Wimbledon

THE MOST EXCITING MATCHES are the ones you win. Every tennis player knows that. Especially nowadays when the world has demonstrably divided itself into winners and losers. Ask any competitor about her most exciting match and it'll be the one where she smashed her opponent into oblivion for the biggest title, in front of the biggest audience, for the biggest number of megabucks. Then ask Evonne Goolagong. She'll tell you about her US Open final against Billie Jean King in 1974. Big title, big audience, big megabucks. But Evonne lost.

'It must have been the most exciting match I've played for atmosphere,' she says enthusiastically. 'We both played great tennis. There have been times when I've played really well and felt I couldn't do anything wrong and I've won. That day, I can still remember during some of the rallies I got goose-bumps. On a few shots the reaction from the crowd was unbelievable. They were going crazy. It was just a wonderful feeling even though I lost.'

She would have been unusual even had she played in a less tough, less professional climate. But Evonne Goolagong was the first new player to emerge after tennis had gone open. She eased the transition. After the grim struggles of the last few years women's tennis suddenly could turn a joyous face to the world. Evonne Goolagong played with a kind of giddy pleasure. She was not playing *for* anything, had no drive for money or power or stardom. She played because she loved it. She made tennis look natural.

In many ways tennis is one of the most unnatural sports. Unless you happen to be ambidextrous like Beverly Baker Fleitz or hit everything with two hands on both sides like Gene Mayer it's an asymetrical activity, emphasising one side of the body over the other. And to compete

149

at the highest level you have to have a combination of skills that don't necessarily go together – aggression but control, power but delicacy, mental concentration that isn't always possible in the midst of free flowing movement. The only way to achieve competence is to practise over and over again. Suzanne Lenlen said it took her six months to develop a backhand at all, two years to have a really good one.

Evonne's natural 'elastic' talent was what thrilled spectators but, 'I had to have some determination to win Wimbledon twice,' says Evonne. 'I think I was just quietly determined.'

Evonne Goolagong in that sense was as manufactured a player as Chris Evert. At the age of thirteen she had been taken from her home in the little Australian bush town of Barellan and brought to Sydney to live in the home of coach Vic Edwards. The poverty of living in a tin shack with her large Aboriginal family – three sisters and two brothers then, with another two brothers born after she left home – was replaced by suburban comfort where she only had to share her bedroom with one other person. Like Margaret Court, another shy country girl, she was uneducated in city manners. Vic Edwards made her have elecution lessons as well as tennis lessons.

But mostly tennis lessons, hours and hours of practising – the backbone of the Edwards coaching method was 'The Drill', where the pupils went through all the elements

Evonne beating her childhood idol
Margaret Court in the 1971 final. A
newspaper cutting of the older
woman was pinned up on the wall
of the tin shack the Goolagongs
lived in at Barellan.

of a stroke but without the ball. There really is no such thing as a natural tennis player. But Evonne had the extra, the flair that made everything she did seem natural. With a player like Chris Evert you could see the seams, see the different component parts of the shot being formed, almost see the signals being sent from the brain as Chris willed her punishing groundstrokes into being. Evonne's strokes seemed to shoot out of her arm, almost as if she couldn't help herself.

She's still in people's minds. She's very memorable for the comparatively light record that she has – she did play plenty of terrible matches in amongst the great ones. But you wanted her to win and you would be watching her. If she played Chris your eyes would be on Evonne the whole time.

Evonne and Chris, like Margaret Court and Billie Jean King before them, had the most dramatic setting of all for their first meeting – the Centre Court at Wimbledon. But where there had been a favourite and an underdog in the previous Australian-American clash, the two younger women went into their 1972 semi-final with much speculation as to who was the better. It was a match with a special aura, the first between these two young women who would, it was assumed – by everybody except Margaret Court and Billie Jean King – dominate the game over the next few years.

That year, 1972, was Evonne's third at Wimbledon but only Chris's first. Chris, with a mind already hard as granite, had advanced far further than Evonne had in her first year. Then she had been overwhelmed by having to play on Centre Court for her very first match, against Peaches Barkowitz. 'I thought it was fine till I got out there,' she recalls. 'But there were so many people. I don't think I towelled off once or had a drink.'

Evonne never thought ahead. It was her weakness and at the same time one of the reasons for her overwhelming popularity with spectators. Tactically superb as she was, all her tennis seemed to be instinctive. There was nothing cold or manipulative or ruthless about it, but because she relied so much on her instincts, she lacked the mental concentration that would have made her into an all time great rather than just a champion. 'On match point or at other key times in a match she was

tough,' said Billie Jean King, who endured Evonne fighting off eight match points before she finally won the 1973 Wimbledon final. 'At other times, though, not so tough. She was mentally lazy, I felt. She could come off with the most unbelievable shots, just slam something off the tips of her toes, and then turn around and miss the easiest shot in the book.'

Journalists, delighted to have her colourful Aboriginal origins to latch on to, said that she went 'walkabout', though in fact the term is now

a derisory one in Australia. The original Aborigines' walkabouts had been over hundreds of miles sometimes in search of better food or conditions. Evonne's were considerably less purposeful. In one match in Dusseldorf, she played dismally for a set and a half, then suddenly began to produce her most sparklingly effective tennis to rampage to victory. She had been trying to remember a tune and only when she finally got it did she realise she was in a tennis match!

This unpredictability must have been heartbreaking for her opponents. She could appear to be completely out of a match, then some spark would ignite inside her and the most exquisite succession of winners would come flaring off her racquet. 'You never knew what to expect,' said Chris Evert. 'And I learned that I couldn't put pressure on myself before playing her because there was nothing I could do.'

Her freedom of movement – she was probably faster than any woman had ever been and certainly as graceful – and the inspirational quality of her play made her seem irresistible when she was in full flow, an unstoppable force that swept across the court like a bush fire. Like Wade and Bueno she drew the spectator's eye, but there was no sense of her being a performer, or imposing her personality as they did. Although she played best before a big crowd she didn't really seem to be aware of the spectators.

She had a beautiful simplicity about her. She was just so natural. There was not a single false thing about her. I have images of her being a child and running around with bare feet and messing around with a tennis ball and having a very sunny sort of personality – people just loved her.

Margaret Court, playing her in the 1971 Wimbledon final, must have found it difficult to counteract the collective yearning for her opponent to win. The older woman, Evonne's heroine in childhood, was clearly nervous. Evonne was not. The then ladies' dressing room attendant Mrs Twynam recalls, 'They all got rather nervous. Even the people looking after them were all on edge. Evonne's the only one I can think of who wasn't all that nervous. She didn't really know what was happening, she was so naïve. She was so fresh and innocent, always singing. She went missing just beforehand and we had to fly out to get hold of her.'

This time Evonne was not afflicted with Centre Court nerves, taking the first set 6–4. She had built

Below: **Evonne and Chris Evert come out for the 1980 final.** *Right:* **there's no mistaking the winner – Evonne's second win gave her greater satisfaction than the first. 'I had something greater to prove,' she says.**

up a 4–0 lead at first until Court's pride had stung her into action. The end of the first set had been hard fought and it seemed the second set would be too. But it was not to be. The older woman did not win another game. She looked tentative and stiff beside Evonne's quicksilver brilliance, unnerved by her opponent's assurance and the ardour of the crowd in supporting her.

Chris Evert was to feel the same mass emotion ranged against her the following year, during their famous semi-final. 'I never resented the fact that the crowds were for Evonne,' she said. 'But I was envious and wanted to shout, "Don't you know I'm feeling something inside?" I was tight-lipped, furiously determined and didn't crack a smile while Evonne laughed at the fact that she sometimes forgot the score.' Evonne won a sparkling match that was considered the best of the tournament. But she had five straight losses to Chris after that.

Unlike Helen Wills, who was criticised for having the killer instinct, Evonne was criticised for not having it. In the next five years she was runner-up at Wimbledon three times, at the US Open four times, twice at the Australian Open and once at the French. Martina Navratilova, who considers Evonne a wonderful champion, has said, 'There are those who sigh when they watch Evonne play and say, "If only she had killer instinct! How much better she could be!" That may be true but it isn't Evonne. It has got to come, ultimately, from within.'

It wasn't in her. If souls are revealed on court then Evonne's was the purest in tennis, light and warm and imbued with luminosity of spirit. She had an inner serenity that made her seem that rarest of beings in a competitive world, a happy person. She swears she does have a temper - 'I can get mad under my

breath,' she says – but few would believe her. She was loved because she was as she seemed, a player whose instinctive genius for tennis left her as sweet, uncomplicated and generous as she had always been.

Although Chris Evert first met her across the net on Wimbledon's Centre Court, she had met her before in person in Dallas's T-Bar-M Racquet Club. The two had been expected to meet in the semi-finals, but Billie Jean King, smarting after a recent 6–1, 6–0 defeat by Chris, had been determined to win this time and did, in three sets. Chris, disliked and feared by the other players, was distressed both by the loss and by the glee of the other women. She walked into the toilets, burst into tears, and was splashing cold water on her face to try and control herself when Evonne came in after her.

'"Don't worry, it's all right,"

Evonne said, patting me softly and putting an arm around my shoulder. "It's just a tennis match, don't worry, don't be upset."'

Tennis as competition was never as important to Evonne as tennis the game and it was not until nine years later, the biggest gap between titles since Bill Tilden, that she again won Wimbledon. By then she had married and had a child, and had also been dogged by injuries that prevented her reaching success at her former level.

Her opponent in the 1980 final was none other than Chris Evert. By then the British crowds had begun to understand the American better – she'd married an Englishman, hadn't she? – and the support was not as one-sided as it once had been. The match was disappointing by both their standards, though played, as always, in the most sporting atmosphere. But Chris was the one who was nervous and tentative, seemingly overwhelmed by the occasion, while Evonne was determined. 'I had something to prove I guess,' she says. 'I'd gone through a lot of injuries and I wasn't just playing for myself any more. I was playing for my family. When I won my first Wimbledon I just thought: that's nice, my first big tournament. But I think you learn to appreciate Wimbledon more as you get older. Winning for the second time meant more to me because I was a lot more professional then.'

But the essence of her remains the same. As she attempts to come back again after the birth of a second child, with still more injury problems, this time from a pelvic weakness, she has matured but not changed from the sunny girl who enchanted audiences all over the world. 'She's just Evonne, that's all,' Rosie Casals said of her. 'Who can be like that? Nobody else I've run into in this life.'

Evonne in 1978 with her thirteen-month-old daughter Kelly. She was the first mother since World War One to win Wimbledon, though Margaret Court always claimed her son Danny had actually appeared on Centre Court – Margaret was pregnant when she lost the 1971 final to Evonne.

14

The First Teenage Prodigy

In 1975, Chris Evert met Billie Jean King in the quarter-finals. Chris lost, and Billie Jean went on to win her sixth Wimbledon singles championship.

THERE CAN'T HAVE BEEN many people in 1971 who didn't understand the meaning of the term 'killer instinct'. It was already a time-honoured concept in sports writing and had been used so many times, in fact, that it was in danger of becoming redundant. But Chris Evert made it sound new-minted. Anyone who hadn't grasped the idea had only to look at that frail sixteen-year-old, thumping hell out of tennis balls and her opponents in the US Open, to get the point. Many players have difficulty, when they get close to the winning post, in closing out a match. They're afraid to win. 'Chris was afraid to lose,' said Billie Jean King.

In a career that stretches back almost half her lifetime, Chris Evert-Lloyd hasn't lost very often. She came into tennis with a mind like granite and carved herself an immortal record that stands comparison with the very best in the sport. Until her shock third round defeat to Kathy Jordan in 1983, she had never finished lower than the semifinals at Wimbledon and had won the title three times. She has won the US Open six times and never finished lower than the semis there either. She has five French titles, countless Virginia Slims and European titles and was the possessor of a clay court winning streak that went 125 matches before she lost to Tracy Austin in Rome. 'She will go down as a tremendous player,' says Margaret Court. 'So many records of winning match tournaments. That alone shows the class of the player. You can't take that away from anybody.'

Even at sixteen Chris Evert played tennis as if it were a mathematical discipline. Her groundstrokes landed the other side of the net with as much precision as if she had drawn a plan of the court on graph paper and lined them all up beforehand. She was unnervingly cool, a robot disguised in a pretty dress but foregoing any pretence at emotion. Tennis as computer game. Audiences, especially in Britain, were cool to her. She could have played against Attila the Hun and they'd have wanted her opponent to win. There was a warm vulnerable teenager underneath the mask but nobody saw her. All they saw was a naked ambition that seemed indecently presumptuous in such a young girl. She was disliked, just as Little Mo had been disliked, not for wanting to win but for wanting to win so much.

Like Maureen Connolly she always looked grimly determined, as if she hated her opponents. Maureen Connolly really did at first but Chris never has. 'You have to have a certain negative feeling when you play someone,' she says now. 'But it's not against that person. It's just a hatred of losing. You have to hate to lose when you're out there. You can't let your emotions get involved when you play. If you've been out to dinner with someone the night before you have to be twice as mentally tough when you play her. The most difficult matches I ever had were with my sister Jeannie when she was on the tour for a while. I felt sick to my stomach going out there and playing her. It's better when I play someone I don't know.'

Sick to her stomach she may have been but she didn't lose to her sister. Killer instinct doesn't let its possessor off the hook, any more than she does her victim. Chris Evert was always in its grip. The daughter of a teaching pro in Fort Lauderdale, Florida, she had been brought up to try her hardest to win. As long as she enjoyed the game and did her best her father didn't mind how she did. Chrissie did. She cared passionately, and took her pride in being the num-

Chrissie's progress in 1973 is watched anxiously by her mother Colette, second row down, far left, and some famous fellow players, among them Billie Jean King and Virginia Wade.

ber one junior into the adult game. 'I got used to being number one,' she says. 'I didn't want to settle for being number five. My father brought me up to try and win and never give up but he never put an emphasis on being number one. I myself didn't want to settle for less.'

Such ruthlessness then, in the days before Austin and Jaeger, seemed remarkable for a teenager. Evert was the first teenage prodigy of the modern era and, it seems, the most durable, still a contender for major titles when some of the younger women are just about finished – bored or injured or just plain burnt out.

This is why Chris's people were very clever with her. People had been talking about her and she suddenly arrived at sixteen and was beating people at that age. They waited until that stage and she came in and beat the top players right from the word go. Whereas Andrea Jaeger and Tracy Austin came in at fourteen. Now there's no way at fourteen you're going to beat the current champion because she's going to be that much stronger than you are, so you come in with a losing record and the memory of that never really leaves you.

Chris Evert started off her career in women's events with a defeat of Margaret Court in her Grand Slam year. She didn't set her sights any lower after that. Chris, despite her Catholic upbringing, was always an embodiment of the Protestant work ethic. The American Dream girl – if you work hard enough you'll get to the top. She 'looks easy to play against', said Billie Jean King. 'She puts very little spin on her ground-strokes – just a little topspin on her backhand and a little slice on her forehand. Her service is hardly awe-

Chris Evert's hairstyle and dress often changed but her determination was always there.

some; she just wants to get the ball in play. One other problem is a slight lack of mobility, which has kept her from developing a really solid net game.

'It's all deceptive – her ground-strokes are so stunning and her anticipation so uncanny that they make up for almost all her deficiencies.'

Hers was a very modern success story but in many ways Chris Evert was a throwback to the stars of an earlier period. In the world as re-created by Margaret Court and Billie Jean King, any girl who couldn't serve and volley was a sissy. Chris was a great baseliner, the first to dominate the game since Maureen Connolly, and she reminded people of what the so-called feminine game

was all about. Lambert Chambers, Lenglen, Wills and Betz had all extolled the virtues of the drive over the volley. Chris, as the women's movement slashed and volleyed its way forward, seemed to prove the older generation's point.

She seemed too to *be* an old-fashioned girl. As women in the seventies cropped their hair and donned their dungarees, Chris emphasised her feminity with coloured trims on her dresses, jewellery on court and a ladylike demeanour. Older women like Billie Jean had fought to be seen as athletes first, women second. But Chris always wanted it the other way round. She once said no point was worth falling over for, and luckily for her, she was good enough not to have to.

Right: **Chris Evert's emergence as a teenage superstar spawned a whole generation of indomitable baseliners with double-handed backhands, like Andrea Jaeger** (*far right*).

Whether Wimbledon was sunny, as in 1983, or rainy, as in 1980, the crowds always came.

But alongside her demure, defiantly traditional feminity was an aggression, a toughness in competition that made many male tennis players of the seventies look like seven-stone weaklings. As they choked and folded their way to defeat, Chris Evert 'hung tough' as the Americans put it, at the same time looking fresh and neat and pretty and unthreatening to the male ego.

Chris's mind on the court was definitely the strongest out of all the great champions I've played. Even stronger than Billie Jean because it was much more stable. I've seen Billie Jean playing lots of bad matches but she was an amazing champion who had a knack of psyching herself up for major championships. I almost never saw Chris playing a bad match.

The bad matches she has played have been, unfortunately, mostly in Wimbledon finals. At the age of twenty-one she had already won the championship twice – in 1974 and 1976 – and was indisputably the world's number one woman tennis player. But her domination of the women's game was not reflected in her Wimbledon record after that. She was beaten in the 1977 semi-finals; then she was in three losing finals in a row, two to Martina Navratilova and one to Evonne Goolagong Cawley. Having built a reputation on her imperturbability and determination, she has seemed strangely tentative at Wimbledon, lacking the nerveless self-belief that made her seem invulnerable elsewhere.

It was not that she couldn't play on grass. Her critics have said she is neither mobile nor varied enough for the surface, but her two classic finals against Martina Navratilova at Eastbourne – she won one and lost one – showed that she could play on anything. Wimbledon, though, is the one tournament she is in awe of, and her mental assets of concentration and willpower were eroded by that. 'It's bigger than the players,' she says, 'and very few of the tournaments are.' There was a gap of five years before she won her most recent title there, in 1981 against Hana Mandlikova. That day it was Hana who found everything was bigger than she was and the match was disappointingly one-sided, as so many women's finals have been in recent years.

By Chris's own high standards the last few years have been disappointing, though since 1974 there has not been a year when she has not won a Grand Slam title. It is a measure of

Left: **Hana Mandlikova, one of the few teenage stars to play the all court game, perhaps because her role model was the attacking game of Martina Navratilova. But in the 1981 final the occasion and Chris Evert-Lloyd's steadiness at the baseline were too much for her.**

her greatness that it is comparative failure for her only to win one in a year. She has become acknowledged as the world's number two player, overshadowed at the age of twenty-nine by Martina Navratilova.

She has a far superior record to Martina because she was such a young peaker. She held off Martina's challenge for a long time and now I think she has finally thought, well, number two is just too easy for her to stay at.

In a way Chris Evert-Lloyd is proof that a human being can survive just about anything. She's come through the trauma of being a teen-age prodigy and growing up in the public eye, then of being number one and a target for everybody to shoot down. But she has also survived the traumas of the women's fight to establish their game in the open era. She has succeeded admirably in coping with all the pressure, public and personal – but only she knows what tennis has cost her.

Many of today's younger players, being subjected to similar stresses, are coping less gracefully and – perhaps wanting to cushion themselves emotionally – have chosen other priorities. 'They've all got managers and agents and coaches and parents, who all see the money signs much more. The emphasis is on the money, not on the titles,' says Chris. She hungered for the titles, aiming always for the highest level, which entails laying yourself open to the greatest disappointment and pain when you lose. That process is the real adventure in sport and it doesn't matter whether you conduct it from the baseline or the net. Chris Evert-Lloyd was seen as careful, safe, defensive, but emotionally she was as

Tracy Austin had Chris Evert's style and will to win but she may have done too much too soon. She was twice US champion before she was twenty but in recent years she has been plagued by injury.

much of an adventurer on court as Billie Jean or Margaret or any of them.

Determination may last for ever but after a while it becomes difficult to maintain the spirit of adventure, the passion underpinning the enterprise. 'It's just that I think I started earlier than anybody else,' sighs Chris. 'I didn't start when I was twenty-one. I started really at fifteen, sixteen and therefore mentally sometimes I question: Do I really need this? What am I doing this again for?'

That question, that doubt as to whether she really wants to be out

on the court at all, has made few inroads into the basic consistency of her game. In fact she moves faster than she used to and has greatly improved not only the technical quality of her volleying but also her ability to change the pattern of the game from baseline to net. But at the highest level, against her great rival Martina Navratilova, she has looked uncommitted, not as assertive mentally as she used to be. As the former Czech's game has come to its full, awesome maturity, Chris has lost her strongest weapon, the burning compulsion to win that turns a competitor into a killer.

'I feel that Martina's hungrier,' she admits. 'I've been ranked number one in the world seven times. That's what's hard for me, to get hungry for every match. I think that right now, in the last two or three years, Martina's started to play her best tennis. But for five or six years she was always just number three or number four in the world. She never really made it. She has more to prove at this point than I do. The difference is, she's been hungrier to win than I have over the last couple of years. And I do feel I'm not as single-minded as I used to be.'

It could not have been otherwise. She has matured both as a woman and as a player. The tunnel vision of early days has been replaced with a broader outlook on life as she has

Left: **Jo Durie, now Britain's number one player, has an aggressive all court game.**
Right: **Chris Evert. At the age of thirty she may find herself more and more under pressure from the Duries of the world.**

taken on both emotional and political responsibilities. She was president of the Women's Tennis Association in 1984, a position she had held once before in 1976 without anybody actually noticing. 'I was more of a figurehead then,' she confesses. 'I didn't really get involved or participate in that many things.' This time she has been an active president, working hard to show the younger players what the WTA can do to help them.

Her personal life expanded too when she married British Davis Cup player John Lloyd, though if her emotional security has, as it now appears, been dissolving for some time, it must have had a great effect on this woman whose strongest sporting asset is her brain. Only she knows what tennis has cost her.

Despite her recent stresses and strains, she is about to relaunch herself as a serious challenger to Martina Navratilova. She is as far ahead of the other women as Navratilova is currently ahead of her so it would be easy to settle for number two. But Chris has been undergoing strenuous physical fitness training, she's sharpening her volleying technique, she's experimenting with a midsize racquet. 'Looking back at history,' she says, 'I'm learning that Billie Jean, Margaret Court, Evonne all seemed to peak in their late twenties, early thirties. I don't think I've seen my best tennis.'

A prospect to delight the Centre Court, if not Martina Navratilova.

Chris Evert-Lloyd after her shock third round defeat to Kathy Jordan at the 1983 Wimbledon. She denied reports that she was ill but had to leave a press conference hurriedly in order to be sick. It was the first time she had failed to reach the semi-finals of a major event.

15

Staking a Claim to Greatness

IF YOU WERE TO PROGRAMME a computer with all the elements that you'd need for a woman tennis champion in that resonant year, 1984, it would have to come up with the name of Martina Navratilova. An exiled Czech who has embraced the most capitalist country in the world: a woman with the strength of a man and as little body fat as a man; a woman whose sexuality by her own admission encompasses both male and female, a player whose life is controlled by her computer; a person whose motives remain mysterious behind her open lifestyle.

As a tennis player Martina Navratilova has everything. She is strong – stronger even than Margaret Court, says Evonne Cawley. She has a lean muscular build – light and finely tuned as a racing bike. She is athletic, an easy mover round the court and supple in reaching for the shots that seem just out of reach. She has every shot in the book and is working on the sequel. She even has the quality she lacked for so long, the self-belief of the champion. She seems a freak of nature, the perfect tennis player.

But though Martina has natural gifts in abundance she has not just

arrived at her freakish level of perfection. In the 1980s even marking time on the women's tennis circuit means you have to work. This is not to say that the modern women are better than the players of twenty or even fifty years ago. Then there was just as much raw talent – in many periods even more than there is today. But no tennis players have pushed themselves to the extremes of today's stars. None have had access to the wealth of technical, psychological, nutritional and scientific knowledge that is on offer to modern sportsmen and women. 'They study the whole game much more than we did,' says Kay Stammers, Britain's losing finalist to the great Alice Marble in 1939. 'They work harder. They study the game and their opponents much more than we did.'

The world of sport is possibly more democratic now that television has come into every home and you can actually see that sporting legends are real people and not the gods and goddesses who people the creative writing pages at the back of the newspaper.

The players today feel, as people do in all of life now, that they have the opportunity of winning or doing well and they are prepared to work. I think in the past people accepted that, well, this was their lot and it was someone else's lot that they happened to be good. They were more satisfied with the idea of people all being at different levels.

Now the only level that means anything in women's tennis is number one. And all the players think they can get there, from the tiny two-handed tots to the tiny two-handed teenagers, particularly in America, the land built on a promise – if you work hard enough you'll get what you want. Europeans, whose experience mostly tells them the opposite, have always been desperate enough for the wealth on offer in the States to abandon their perception that life is inherently unfair. Most have got only the work. Mar-

tina Navratilova didn't see that part at all at first. She saw only the second half of the promise – you'll get what you want.

The West was what Martina wanted, all of it, hamburgers and pizzas and fresh milk, her stepfather's pay for two days measured out in grocery items. Television and American football and Gucci leather bags. She didn't even mind when she put on twenty pounds in three weeks. She thought she looked more feminine that way, a culturally conditioned view of her own body image that she would reject later in favour of the leaner, meaner model she has now.

Most of all though, Martina wanted freedom. 'There's a political freedom in America that you don't have in many countries,' she says. 'But that's not what I liked about the country. I valued the freedom to do as you pleased when you pleased. I wanted it to be my choice of where I would play tennis and how much I wanted to play tennis. At home the

Above: **Chris Lloyd demonstrates her generous sportsmanship as she acknowledges Martina's ecstasy at her first Wimbledon victory – which perhaps meant more to her than any other.**

Right: **Better two racquets than one, even if they are the two best backhand volleyers in the game! Martina with Billie Jean King on their way to the ladies doubles title in 1979. This was the twentieth title that Billie Jean needed to break Elizabeth Ryan's record and Martina said she herself was more nervous for it than for any of her own singles matches.**

tennis federation, the sports federation, the school people were all telling me what I should be doing. I found it difficult to concentrate on tennis when you didn't know whether you would get to play again. I wanted somewhere where I didn't have anybody telling me what to do.'

Martina Navratilova adapted so well to American life because she is an individualist, temperamentally suited to seeing herself as a number one. Because she has surrounded herself with a team of helpers, coaches, nutritionist, computer and co., she is often regarded as a dependent person, but this is to ignore the

fact that the people around her are all devoted to the cause of her success. She's the queen bee, with a bunch of workers swarming around her.

When she came to the West originally she was obviously a potential star. Raw talent exploded out of her – as indeed did raw temper. Martina was mean and moody in those days. Magnificence came later. On the court though she always gave signs of what was to come. Christine Truman Janes played her only once. 'It was her first Wimbledon and my last. It was the first round and I lost. Even at sixteen, as

she was then, she was terrifically talented. Now I think she's going to be one of the best tennis players ever. She's exceptionally good and would have been good in anybody's time.'

Or in any country. There seems no reason why Navratilova could not have succeeded in her aim of becoming the world's best tennis player had she stayed in her home country. Czechoslovakia has one of the finest squad systems in the world, though the recent stars have seemed to fail mentally at the very highest level: Ivan Lendl with his inability to land a Grand Slam title, Hana Mandlikova with her unpredictable results.

Martina Navratilova is currently playing the greatest tennis of her life but she has not yet carved out a reputation as an all time great. 'I have to be around for a couple more years yet,' she admits. But if her actual record does not yet stand comparison with the very best, her tennis certainly does.

I think what happens is that in the Iron Curtain countries there is such a policy of black market that people don't always derive things by totally honest means. If you do well on a level that people can acknowledge, then you are spoilt rotten. You're given much more than anybody else. I think it eliminates a whole lot of the process of climbing up the ladder. They always tend to be a little spoilt, a little disdainful, a little aloof, not really prepared to knuckle down and work, and not really being brought up to be respectful. They've won everything so easily and suddenly they're put in a situation where they want something

very badly. A player like Jimmy Connors will have come through every stage, fighting all the way, in every match he plays. So when it comes to the crunch they haven't been doing that all the time and he has. When it comes to the crunch they're still babies.

Lady Diana Spencer, shortly to become the Princess of Wales, with the Duchess of Kent, enjoying the 1981 Wimbledon. *Right:* **Chris Evert Lloyd, champion that year** (*inset*), **specially requested, and was granted, a meeting with the future princess. In 1983 she went out in the third round, but it wasn't for lack of effort.**

Martina, if the truth be told, often was. She had more power, more speed, and more natural talent than Chris but she consistently lost to her. Some put it down to a lack of concentration, the Czech version of Goolagong's so-called walkabouts. Others thought that she was insecure emotionally – as indeed anyone would have been in a position of self exile – and lacked confidence. Martina herself has defined it as the difference between killer instinct and competitiveness – the competitor wants to win but the person with killer instinct wants to humiliate opponents. 'I didn't want to beat people badly because I felt sorry for them,' says Martina. 'If I'm winning 5-0 now I don't hesitate but before I'd maybe lose a game on purpose. Now I still feel bad but I'm more willing to beat them thoroughly.'

Even at the 1978 Wimbledon when she won her first major title, she did not have killer instinct. In the semi-finals she was up against Evonne Cawley, who had been suffering for some time from an ankle injury. Evonne, playing brilliant touch tennis that was as disciplined as it was inspired, had won the first set, and in the third was within a point of leading 4–3 when she finally strained the ankle completely reaching for a Navratilova lob. She gave a little cry of pain and from then on was unable to move off one foot. Even when she is standing still it is impossible to prevent Mrs Cawley making winners, but Martina had only to make no mistakes for the match to be hers. It was, but only after Martina, obviously sorry for her opponent, had fluffed so many shots that even the sunny Evonne looked irritated.

That 1978 Wimbledon was Martina's almost by default. Chris Evert had temporarily mislaid her killer instinct and failed to close out the final after being 5-4 up in the third

Left: Martina Navratilova on her way to a fourth Wimbledon championship in 1983. Officials and ball boys line up to applaud as Martina is presented with the trophy by the Duke of Kent, and (*far right*) her victory smile says it all.

Right: Chris and Martina, two of the most sporting players the game has ever seen, just before their 1982 final.

Martina Navratilova on the run with a football, and, opposite, Virginia Wade in 1983, still taking her shots on the run.

set. But 1979 was convincingly Navratilova's year, her aggressive skills knocking Chris's classic ones over like skittles in a bowling alley. This time there was no doubt – Martina was the best player in the world. That year she also won the doubles with Billie Jean, who had finally reached her record twenty titles.

Billie Jean had been one of the players Martina had admired as a child, mainly because she confirmed her belief that serve and volley was the way to play tennis. Her stepfather had tried to instil the virtues of groundstrokes and steady play into her, but Martina, even then her own person, was not impressed. Playing with Billie Jean taught her

the other side of the equation that had drawn her unwittingly to America. Work hard and you'll get what you want. 'She had such a drive that she makes you work harder,' says Martina. 'I wanted to. I thought, if this woman can do it I can do it. She didn't change my game though she did help me technically. She did make me realise, though, that I was capable of being the best but I had to put out the work, no matter how talented I was.'

It was a lesson Martina forgot for a while, losing her number one world ranking in 1980 and 1981 to Chris Lloyd. 'You get complacent and don't work as hard because you think you don't need it,' she says.

'You're more willing to work hard when you're getting there.' There were also other pressures. The publicity surrounding her self-confessed lesbian affairs was overwhelming and Martina seemed quite unprepared mentally for it. Her parents had returned to Czechoslovakia after a period of trying to live in the US to be with her. The emotional problems she has had to deal with, in fact, have been unique.

To lead her out of her personal and professional wilderness and into the promised land (you'll get what you want) Martina assembled a team of helpers who seemed an oddball collection but who were actually very skilled in their different ways. Nancy Lieberman, a pro basketball player, sharpened her aggression. Renée Richards, who had made history as the first trans-sexual tennis player, sharpened her strategy and her self-confidence, teaching her she could win even when not at her best. And then there was Robert Haas, the computer man.

The computer has been a mixed blessing for Martina – people seem to think she is just one of the programmes it turns out. Robert Haas, ridiculed as the 'nitwit nutritionist' by Renée Richards, reinforced this image of Martina by saying she would be the first bionic tennis player. What he failed to say was that one thousand other people were helped by his computer, ordinary people who wanted to lose weight or change to a healthier diet. It never was Martina's personal property. 'I have to put in the work myself,' she

says. 'The computer can't hit fore-hands for you. I'm the one who has to go out there and run, lift weights, play basketball, whatever. It's annoying if people think that's what makes me a better player. It's not the reason I've won a lot of matches. You can give the same information to other players and they won't be able to do anything with it.'

What she has done is stake a claim to greatness. In 1982 she took Wimbledon and the French, which she had never won. In 1983 she took Wimbledon and the US title which she had never won. She so completely dominates the game that her rare losses become media events, with experts proferring their explanations of the psychological reasons for her defeat. It is still commonly believed that Martina has a mental weakness and that if anybody could manage to come close to her physically she might succumb to pressure. This theory is extremely difficult to test out as Martina has lost only a handful of matches over the past couple of years. In the whole of 1983, for example, she had only one defeat – by American teenager Kathy Horvath in the French Open.

That one defeat was clearly traumatic for Martina, an experience she had forgotten how to deal with. Before the tournament was over she had sacked Renée Richards, ostensibly for not giving enough time to the job.

She has always been a little easy come, easy go, certainly with money, possessions and people. She is very emotional but it's easy come, easy go emotion. Last year when she won the US Open, which is all that was left for her, she was ecstatic for half an hour. You see her later and she's talking about something different. That's possibly what she conveys on the court. It's just a job well done and she doesn't have any really deep emotions. She

doesn't have the memory so how can you?

Martina, phenomenal machine? Or merely Martina the champion, moving on mentally to the next match, the next tournament, afraid of becoming complacent again? 'I would like to be one of the greatest of all time,' she says, 'but I've not done enough. I'll have to be around for a couple more years yet. But the higher the level you reach the shorter you can keep it up. I would have said two or three years ago that I could have kept up for twenty years. Now I don't know. Maybe six months, maybe six years.'

The one certain thing is that as the months and years go on she will be challenged more and more and the mental pressure will become greater and greater. 'She certainly has to rank among the very great

players,' says Helen Jacobs, still watching tennis even if no longer playing it. 'But one waits to see how she can hold up. That's the test of the very greatest players, how long they can sustain their game. The pressure gets heavier as time goes on.'

They are all there waiting, in classrooms all over the world, to take over from Martina. As tennis becomes ever more glamorous at the top, ever more accessible to ordinary people at the bottom, more and more girls want to be Martina or want to be Chrissie when they grow up. Whether the game today can deliver those young hopefuls safely into adulthood remains to be seen.

1983, and Martina triumphs for the fourth time, beating Andrea Jaeger in a final that showed her complete domination of the game. Her cardigan is safely on this time – in 1979 she refused to give in to photographers' requests that she cover up her muscles.

It's so unhealthy just now. There are all these agents wanting to make sure they get a piece of the action so they go in there like hawks recruiting the youngsters if they show any promise. They offer them tremendous guarantees. I know that with some of the promising sixteen and seventeen-year-olds, they are offering a guarantee of $120,000 dollars for the first year. Now this is at sixteen years old. It's pretty hard for someone to refuse that. Suddenly these kids think that they're huge successes but they're not mature enough to cope with it and not *really good enough either because they can't come up with the consistency at that stage. In order to develop naturally obviously you're going to have to put up with the pressures, but you don't want all those added things.*

The pressures have always been there, from Maud Watson nearing the end of her fifty-five match winning streak; to Suzanne Lenglen, almost hysterical with nerves sometimes; to Martina Navratilova, the champion in exile, the woman whose real home is neither in the country of her birth nor the glossy, vulgar city of her adoption, Dallas, but on the tennis court. Within this enclosed space, imposing a discipline that she *will* accept, her richest dramas are played out, her deepest feelings displayed to watching and not always generous eyes.

In recreating herself as a champion for the second time round Martina Navratilova has burned herself into the memory now. Proud, perplexing, sometimes difficult in the past, she has become surer within herself, a great champion to lead women's tennis into the brave new world of its second century at Wimbledon. Beyond those rectangular strips of turf, bounded by white lines, the managers and coaches and parents and agents hover, ready to trap the immature and unwary with open chequebooks and flattering words. But all these things are superfluous. Right from the beginnings of the sport, through all its great players, champions and competitors alike, all that matters is the beauty and excitement of the battle. And the soul on court.

The Championship Roll

1884   Miss M. Watson d Miss L. Watson (6–8 6–3 6–3)
1885   Miss M. Watson d Miss B. Bingley (6–1 7–5)
1886   Miss B. Bingley d Miss M. Watson (6–3 6–3)
1887   Miss C. Dod d Miss B. Bingley (6–2 6–0)
1888   Miss C. Dod d Mrs G.W. Hillyard (6–3 6–3)
1889   Mrs G.W. Hillyard d Miss H.B.G. Rice (4–6 8–6 6–4)
1890   Miss H.B.G. Rice d Miss M. Jacks (6–4 6–1)
1891   Miss C. Dod d Mrs G.W. Hillyard (6–2 6–1)
1892   Miss C. Dod d Mrs G.W. Hillyard (6–1 6–1)
1893   Miss C. Dod d Mrs G.W. Hillyard (6–8 6–1 6–4)
1894   Mrs G.W. Hillyard d Miss L. Austin (6–1 6–1)
1895   Miss C. Cooper d Miss H. Jackson (7–5 8–6)
1896   Miss C. Cooper d Mrs W.H. Pickering (6–2 6–3)
1897   Mrs G.W. Hillyard d Miss C. Cooper (5–7 7–5 6–2)
1898   Miss C. Cooper d Miss L. Martin (6–4 6–4)
1899   Mrs G.W. Hillyard d Miss C. Cooper (6–2 6–3)
1900   Mrs G.W. Hillyard d Miss C. Cooper (4–6 6–4 6–4)
1901   Mrs A. Sterry d Mrs G.W. Hillyard (6–2 6–2)
1902   Miss M.E. Robb d Mrs A. Sterry (7–5 6–1)
1903   Miss D.K. Douglass d Miss E.W. Thomson (4–6 6–4 6–2)
1904   Miss D.K. Douglass d Mrs A. Sterry (6–0 6–3)
1905   Miss M. Sutton (U S) d Miss D.K. Douglass (6–3 6–4)
1906   Miss D.K. Douglass d Miss M. Sutton (U S) (6–3 9–7)
1907   Miss M. Sutton (U S) d Mrs R. Lambert Chambers (6–1 6–4)
1908   Mrs A. Sterry d Miss A.M. Morton (6–4 6–4)
1909   Miss D.P. Boothby d Miss A.M. Morton (6–4 4–6 8–6)
1910   Mrs R. Lambert Chambers d Miss D.P. Boothby (6–2 6–2)
1911   Mrs R. Lambert Chambers d Miss D.P. Boothby (6–0 6–0)
1912   Mrs D.R. Larcombe d Mrs A. Sterry (6–3 6–1)
1913   Mrs R. Lambert Chambers d Mrs R.J. McNair (6–0 6–4)
1914   Mrs R. Lambert Chambers d Mrs D.R. Larcombe (7–5 6–4)
1915–1918 not held
1919   Mlle S. Lenglen (F) d Mrs R. Lambert Chambers (10–8 4–6 9–7)
1920   Mlle S. Lenglen (F) d Mrs R. Lambert Chambers (6–3 6–0)
1921   Mlle S. Lenglen (F) d Miss E. Ryan (U S) (6–2 6–0)
1922   Mlle S. Lenglen (F) d Mrs F.I. Mallory (U S) (6–2 6–0)
1923   Mlle S. Lenglen (F) d Miss K. McKane (6–2 6–2)
1924   Miss K. McKane d Miss H.N. Wills (U S) (4–6 6–4 6–4)

1925 Mlle S. Lenglen (F) d Miss J. Fry (6–2 6–0)

1926 Mrs L.A. Godfree d Sta E. de Alvarez (S P) (6–2 4–6 6–3)

1927 Miss H.N. Wills (U S) d Sta E. de Alvarez (S P) (6–2 6–4)

1928 Miss H.N. Wills (U S) d Sta E. de Alvarez (S P) (6–2 6–3)

1929 Miss H.N. Wills (U S) d Miss H.H. Jacobs (U S) (6–1 6–2)

1930 Mrs F.S. Moody (U S) d Miss E. Ryan (U S) (6–2 6–2)

1931 Frl C. Aussem (G) d Frl H. Krahwinkel (G) (6–2 7–5)

1932 Mrs F.S. Moody (U S) d Miss H.H. Jacobs (U S) (6–3 6–1)

1933 Mrs F.S. Moody (U S) d Miss D.E. Round (6–4 6–8 6–3)

1934 Miss D.E. Round d Miss H.H. Jacobs (U S) (6–2 5–7 6–3)

1935 Mrs F.S. Moody (U S) d Miss H.H. Jacobs (6–3 3–6 7–5)

1936 Miss H.H. Jacobs (U S) d Fru S. Sperling (D E N) (6–2 4–6 7–5)

1937 Miss D.E. Round d Mlle J. Jedrzejowska (6–2 2–6 7–5)

1938 Mrs F.S. Moody (U S) d Miss H.H. Jacobs (U S) (6–4 6–0)

1939 Miss A. Marble (U S) d Miss K.E. Stammers (6–2 6–0)

1940–1945 not held

1946 Miss P.M. Betz (U S) d Miss A.L. Brough (U S) (6–2 6–4)

1947 Miss M.E. Osborne (U S) d Miss D.J. Hart (U S) (6–2 6–4)

1948 Miss A.L. Brough (U S) d Miss D.J. Hart (U S) (6–3 8–6)

1949 Miss A.L. Brough (U S) d Mrs W.D. Du Pont (U S) (10–8 1–6 10–8)

1950 Miss A.L. Brough (U S) d Mrs W.D. Du Pont (U S) (6–1 3–6 6–1)

1951 Miss D.J. Hart (U S) d Miss S.J. Fry (U S) (6–1 6–0)

1952 Miss M. Connolly (U S) d Miss A.L. Brough (U S) (7–5 6–3)

1953 Miss M. Connolly (U S) d Miss D.J. Hart (U S) (8–6 7–5)

1954 Miss M. Connolly (U S) d Miss A.L. Brough (U S) (6–2 7–5)

1955 Miss A.L. Brough (U S) d Mrs J. Fleitz (U S) (7–5 8–6)

1956 Miss S.J. Fry (US) d Miss A. Buxton (6–3 6–1)

1957 Miss A. Gibson (U S) d Miss D.R. Hard (U S) (6–3 6–2)

1958 Miss A. Gibson (U S) d Miss A. Mortimer (8–6 6–2)

1959 Miss M.E. Bueno (B R A) d Miss D.R. Hard (U S) (6–4 6–3)

1960 Miss M.E. Bueno (B R A) d Miss S. Reynolds (S A) (8–6 6–0)

1961 Miss A. Mortimer d Miss C.C. Truman (4–6 6–4 7–5)

1962 Mrs J.R. Susman (U S) d Mrs C. Sukova (C Z) (6–4 6–4)

1963 Miss M. Smith (A U S) d Miss B.J. Moffitt (U S) (6–3 6–4)

1964 Miss M.E. Bueno (B R A) d Miss M. Smith (A U S) (6–4 7–9 6–3)

1965 Miss M. Smith (A U S) d Miss M.E. Bueno (B R A) (6–4 7–5)

1966 Mrs L.W. King (U S) d Miss M.E. Bueno (B R A) (6–3 3–6 6–1)

1967 Mrs L.W. King (U S) d Mrs P.F. Jones (6–3 6–4)

1968 Mrs L.W. King (U S) d Miss J.A.M. Tegart (A U S) (9–7 7–5)

1969 Mrs P.F. Jones d Mrs L.W. King (U S) (3–6 6–3 6–2)

1970 Mrs B.M. Court (A U S) d Mrs L.W. King (U S) (14–12 11–9)

1971	Miss E.F. Goolagong (AUS) d Mrs B.M. Court (6–4 6–1)
1972	Mrs L.W. King (US) d Miss E.F. Goolagong (AUS) (6–3 6–3)
1973	Mrs L.W. King (US) d Miss C.M. Evert (US) (6–0 7–5)
1974	Miss C.M. Evert (US) d Mrs O. Morozova (USSR) (6–0 6–4)
1975	Mrs L.W. King (US) d Mrs R.A. Cawley (AUS) (6–0 6–1)
1976	Miss C.M. Evert (US) d Mrs R.A. Cawley (AUS) (6–3 4–6 8–6)
1977	Miss S.V. Wade d Miss B.F. Stove (NTH) (4–6 6–3 6–1)
1978	Miss M. Navratilova (CZ) d Miss C.M. Evert (US) (2–6 6–4 7–5)
1979	Miss M. Navratilova (CZ) d Mrs J.M. Lloyd (US) (6–4 6–4)
1980	Mrs R.A. Cawley (AUS) d Mrs J.M. Lloyd (US) (6–1 7–6)
1981	Mrs J.M. Lloyd (US) d Miss H. Mandlikova (CZ) (6–2 6–2)
1982	Miss M. Navratilova (US) d Mrs J.M. Lloyd (US) (6–1 3–6 6–2)
1983	Miss M. Navratilova (US) d Miss A. Jaeger (US) (6–0 6–3)

Biographical Records

AUSSEM, Cilly

Later Contessa F.M. Della Corta Brae (married 1936).
Born 4 January 1909, Cologne, Germany.
Died 22 March 1963, Portafino, Genoa, Italy.
Singles 1931.
Other successes:
French Championships, singles 1931; mixed 1930.
German Championships, singles 1927, 1930, 1931; mixed 1928, 1935.

BETZ, Pauline May

Later Mrs R. Addie (married 1949).
Born 6 August 1919, Dayton, Ohio, USA.
Singles 1946.
Other successes:
US Championships, singles 1942, 1943, 1944, 1946.
French Championships, mixed 1946.
Member US Wightman Cup team 1946.
Became a professional in 1947. Graduate Colombia University.

BINGLEY, Blanche, *see* **HILLYARD, Mrs G.W.**

BOOTHBY, Penelope Dora Harvey

Later Mrs A.C. Geen (married 1914).
Born 2 August 1881, Finchley, Middlesex, England.
Died 22 February 1970, Hammersmith, London, England.

Singles 1909.
Doubles 1913.
All England Badminton mixed champion 1909.

BROUGH, Althea Louise

Later Mrs A.T. Clapp (married 1958).
Born 11 March 1923, Oklahoma City, Oklahoma, USA.
Singles 1948, 1949, 1950, 1955.
Doubles 1946, 1948, 1949, 1950, 1954.
Mixed 1946, 1947, 1948, 1950.
Other successes:
US Championships, singles 1947; doubles 1942, 1943, 1944, 1945, 1946, 1947, 1948, 1949, 1950, 1955, 1956, 1957; mixed 1942, 1947, 1948, 1949.
French Championships, doubles 1946, 1947, 1949.
Australian Championships, singles 1950; doubles 1950.
Member US Wightman Cup team 1946–57, winning 22 from 22 rubbers; captain 1956.

BUENO, Maria Esther Andion

Born 11 October 1939, São Paulo, Brazil.
Singles 1959, 1960, 1964.
Doubles 1958, 1960, 1963, 1965, 1966.
Other successes:
US Championships, singles 1959, 1963, 1964, 1966; doubles 1960, 1962, 1966, 1968.

French Championships, doubles 1960; mixed 1960.
Australian Championships, doubles 1960.
Italian Championships, singles 1958, 1961, 1965; doubles 1962.

CAWLEY, Mrs Roger

Formerly Evonne Fay Goolagong (married 1975).
Born 31 July 1951, Barellan, N S W, Australia.
Singles 1971, 1980.
Doubles 1974.
Other successes:
French Championships, singles 1971; mixed 1972.
Australian Championships, singles 1974, 1975, 1976; doubles 1971, 1974, 1975, 1976.
Italian Championships, singles 1973.
Member Australian Federation Cup team 1971-6, 1982.

CHAMBERS, Mrs Robert Lambert

Formerly Dorothea Katharine Douglass (married 1907).
Born 3 September 1878, Ealing, Middlesex, England.
Died 7 January 1960, Kensington, London, England.
Singles 1903, 1904, 1906, 1910, 1911, 1913, 1914.
Other successes:
Wimbledon non-championship doubles 1903, 1907.
Wimbledon non-championship mixed 1906, 1908, 1910.
Olympic gold medal 1908.
Member British Wightman Cup team 1925-6; captain British Wightman Cup team 1924, 1925, 1926.
All England Badminton doubles champion 1903; mixed champion 1904.
Middlesex hockey player. Became a professional in 1928.

CONNOLLY, Maureen Catherine

Later Mrs Norman Brinker (married 1955).
Born 17 September 1934, San Diego, California, U S A.
Died 21 June 1969, Dallas, Texas, U S A.
Singles 1952, 1953, 1954.
Other successes:
U S Championships, singles 1951, 1952, 1953.
French Championships, singles 1953, 1954; doubles 1954; mixed 1954.
Australian Championships, singles 1953; doubles 1953.
Italian Championships, singles 1954.
Member U S Wightman Cup team 1952-4, winning nine out of nine rubbers.
Became a professional in 1955, her amateur career having ended when she broke her leg while horse riding in 1954. She was the first woman to win the 'Grand Slam' and was never beaten in the singles at Wimbledon.

COOPER, Charlotte, *see* STERRY, Mrs A.

COURT, Mrs Barry M., MBE

Formerly Margaret Smith (married 1967).
Born 16 July 1942, Albury, N S W, Australia.
Singles 1963, 1965, 1970.
Doubles 1964, 1969.
Mixed 1963, 1965, 1966, 1968, 1975.
Other successes:
U S Championships singles 1962, 1965, 1969, 1970, 1973; doubles 1963, 1968, 1970, 1973, 1975; mixed 1961, 1962, 1963, 1964, 1965, 1969, 1970, 1972.
French Championships, singles 1962, 1964, 1969, 1970, 1973; doubles 1964, 1965, 1966, 1973; mixed 1963, 1964, 1965, 1969.
Australian Championships, singles 1960, 1961, 1962, 1963, 1964, 1965, 1966, 1969, 1970, 1971, 1973; doubles 1961, 1962, 1963, 1965, 1969, 1970, 1971, 1973; mixed 1963, 1964.
Italian Championships, singles 1962, 1963, 1964; doubles 1963, 1964, 1968; mixed 1961, 1964, 1968.
German Championships, singles 1963, 1964, 1965; doubles 1964, 1965, 1966; mixed 1965, 1966.
South African Championships, singles 1968, 1970, 1971; doubles 1966, 1971; mixed 1966, 1970, 1971, 1974.
Member Australian Federation Cup team 1963-70, winning 20 out of 20 singles, 15 out of 20 doubles.
Unique in the number of major championships won. She won the 'Grand Slam' in singles in 1970, having performed the same feat in mixed doubles in 1963 with Ken Fletcher.

DOD, Charlotte (Lottie)

Born 24 September 1871, Bebington, Cheshire, England.
Died 27 June 1960, Sway, Hampshire, England.
Singles 1887, 1888, 1891, 1892, 1893.
Other successes:
Irish Championships, singles 1887; mixed 1887.
British women's gold champion 1904 (Troon).
English women's hockey international 1899, 1900.
She was never beaten at Wimbledon. The youngest champion in 1887 at the age of 15 years 10 months.

DOUGLASS, Dorothea Katharine, *see* CHAMBERS, Mrs R. Lambert

DU PONT, Mrs W.

Formerly Margaret Evelyn Osborne (married 1947).
Born 4 March 1918, Joseph, Oregon, U S A.
Singles 1947.
Doubles 1946, 1948, 1949, 1950, 1954.
Mixed 1962.
Other successes:
U S Championships, singles 1948, 1949, 1950; doubles
  1941, 1942, 1943, 1944, 1945, 1946, 1947, 1948,
  1949, 1950, 1955, 1956, 1957; mixed 1943, 1944,
  1945, 1946, 1950, 1956, 1958, 1959, 1960.
French Championships, singles 1946, 1949; doubles
  1946, 1947, 1949.
Member U S Wightman Cup team 1946–62, winning
  18 out of 18 rubbers; captain 1953–5, 1957, 1958,
  1961–3, 1965.

EVERT LLOYD, Christine Marie

Formerly Miss Evert (married 1979).
Born 21 December 1954, Fort Lauderdale, Florida,
  U S A.
Singles 1974, 1976, 1981.
Doubles 1976.
Other successes:
U S Championships, singles 1975, 1976, 1977, 1978,
  1980, 1983.
French Championships, singles 1974, 1975, 1979,
  1980, 1983; doubles 1974, 1975.
Italian Championships, singles 1974, 1975, 1980, 1981,
  1982; doubles 1974, 1975.
Australian Championships, singles 1982.
Member of the U S Wightman Cup team 1971–1982.
Member U S Federation Cup team 1977–1982.
Double fisted on the backhand.

FRY, Shirley June

Later Mrs K.E. Irvin (married 1957).
Born 30 June 1927, Akron, Ohio, U S A.
Singles 1956.
Doubles 1951, 1952, 1953.
Mixed 1956.
Other successes:
U S Championships, singles 1956; doubles 1951, 1952,
  1953, 1954.
French Championships, singles 1951; doubles 1950,
  1951, 1952, 1953.
Australian Championships, singles 1957; doubles
  1957.
Italian Championships, doubles 1951; mixed 1951.
Member U S Wightman Cup team 1949–56.

GIBSON, Althea

Later Mrs W.A. Darben (married 1965).
Born 25 August 1927, Silver, South Carolina, U S A.
Singles 1957, 1958.
Doubles 1956, 1957, 1958.
Other successes:
U S Championships, 1957, 1958; mixed 1957.
French Championships, singles 1956; doubles 1956.
Australian Championships, doubles 1957.
Member U S Wightman Cup team 1957–8.
The first black champion. Became a professional in
  1958.

GODFREE, Mrs L.A.

Formerly Kathleen (Kitty) McKane (married 1926).
Born 7 May 1897, Bayswater, London, England.
Singles 1924, 1926.
Mixed 1924, 1926.
Other successes:
U S Championships, doubles 1923, 1927; mixed 1925.
Olympic gold medallist 1920.
Member British Wightman Cup team 1923–34.
All England Badminton champion, singles 1920, 1921,
  1922, 1924; doubles 1921, 1924; mixed 1924, 1925.
  In 1926 she and Leslie Godfree became the only
  married pair to win the Wimbledon mixed doubles
  championship.

GOOLAGONG, Evonne Fay, *see* **CAWLEY, Mrs
Roger**

HANTZE, Karen J., *see* **SUSMAN, Mrs J.R.**

HART, Doris Jane

Born 20 June 1925, St Louis, Missouri, U S A.
Singles 1951.
Doubles 1947, 1951, 1952, 1953.
Mixed 1951, 1952, 1953, 1954, 1955.
Other successes:
U S Championships, singles 1954, 1955; doubles 1951,
  1952, 1953, 1954; mixed 1951, 1952, 1953, 1954,
  1955.
French Championships, singles 1950, 1952; doubles
  1948, 1950, 1951, 1952, 1953; mixed 1951, 1952,
  1953.
Australian Championships, singles 1949; doubles
  1950; mixed 1949, 1950.
Member U S Wightman Cup team 1946–55, winning
  14 out of 14 singles, 8 out of 9 doubles.
Became a professional in 1955.

HILLYARD, Mrs George Whiteside

Formerly Blanche Bingley (married 1887).

Born 3 November 1863, Greenford, Middlesex, England.

Died 6 August 1946, Pulborough, Sussex, England.

Singles 1886, 1889, 1894, 1897, 1899, 1900.

Other successes:

Wimbledon non-championship doubles 1899, 1901, 1906.

German Championships, singles 1897, 1900.

Irish Championships, singles 1888, 1894, 1897; mixed 1894, 1897.

Welsh Championships, singles 1888.

Her husband, Commander (R N) Hillyard was secretary of the All England Club from 1907 to 1924. She completed 24 times in the Championships between 1884 and 1913.

JACOBS, Helen Hull

Born 6 August 1908, Globe, Arizona, U S A.

Singles 1936.

Other successes:

U S Championships, singles 1932, 1933, 1934, 1935; doubles 1932, 1934, 1935; mixed 1934.

Member U S Wightman Cup team 1927–39.

JONES, Mrs P.F. (Ann)

Formerly Adrianne Shirley Haydon (married 1962).

Born 7 October 1938, Birmingham, England.

Singles 1969.

Mixed 1969.

Other successes:

French Championships, singles 1961, 1966; doubles 1963, 1968, 1969.

Italian Championships, singles 1966; doubles 1969.

Member British Wightman Cup team 1957–70, 1975; captain 1971, 1972; British Federation Cup team 1963–7, 1971.

English women's table tennis international 1954–9; English women's doubles champion 1956, 1958.

A left hander.

KING, Mrs L.W. (Billie Jean)

Formerly Billie Jean Moffitt (married 1965).

Born 22 November 1943, Long Beach, California, U S A.

Singles 1966, 1967, 1968, 1972, 1973, 1975.

Doubles 1961, 1962, 1965, 1967, 1968, 1970, 1971, 1972, 1973, 1979.

Mixed 1967, 1971, 1973, 1974.

Other successes:

U S Championships, singles 1967, 1971, 1972, 1974; doubles 1964, 1967, 1974, 1978, 1980; mixed 1967, 1971, 1973, 1976.

French Championships, singles 1972; doubles 1972; mixed 1967, 1970.

Australian Championships, singles 1968; mixed 1968.

Italian Championships, singles 1970; doubles 1970.

German Championships, singles 1971; doubles 1971.

South African Championships, singles 1966, 1967, 1969; doubles 1967, 1970; mixed 1967.

Member U S Wightman Cup team 1961–78; U S Federation Cup team 1963–79; Federation Cup captain 1965, 1976.

LARCOMBE, Mrs D.R.

Formerly Ethel Warneford Thomson (married 1906).

Born 8 June 1879, Islington, Middlesex, England.

Died 11 August 1965, Budleigh Salterton, Devon, England.

Singles 1912.

Mixed 1914.

Other successes:

Wimbledon non-championship doubles 1904, 1905; mixed 1903, 1904, 1912.

Irish Championships, singles 1912; mixed 1912.

Scottish Championships, singles 1910, 1911, 1912; doubles 1910, 1911, 1912; mixed 1910, 1912.

All England Badminton singles champion 1900, 1901, 1903, 1904, 1906; doubles champion 1902, 1904, 1905, 1906; mixed champion 1903, 1906.

Became a professional in 1922. Her husband, Major Dudley Larcombe, was secretary of the All England Club 1925–39.

LENGLEN, Suzanne Rachel Flore

Born 24 May 1899, Compiègne, France.

Died 4 July 1938, Paris, France.

Singles 1919, 1920, 1921, 1922, 1923, 1925.

Doubles 1919, 1920, 1921, 1922, 1923, 1925.

Mixed 1920, 1922, 1925.

Other successes:

French Championships, singles 1925, 1926; doubles 1925, 1926; mixed 1925, 1926.

World Hard Court Championships, singles 1914, 1921, 1922, 1923; doubles 1914, 1921, 1922; mixed 1921, 1922, 1923.

Olympic gold medals (2) 1920.

Became a professional in 1926. Except for her retirement against Molla Mallory at Forest Hills in 1921 she was invincible in singles anywhere from 1919 to 1926. Her standard of achievement was unique. She died of pernicious anaemia.

McKANE, Kathleen (Kitty), *see* **GODFREE, Mrs L.A.**

MARBLE, Alice
Born 28 September 1913, Plumas County, California, USA.
Singles 1939.
Doubles 1938, 1939.
Mixed 1937, 1938, 1939.
Other successes:
US Championships, singles 1936, 1938, 1939, 1940; doubles 1937, 1938, 1939, 1940; mixed 1936, 1938, 1939, 1940.
Member US Wightman Cup team 1933-9.
Became a professional in 1941.

MOFFITT, Billie Jean, *see* **KING, Mrs L.W.**

MOODY, Mrs F.S. (Helen Wills)
Formerly Helen Newington Wills (married 1929).
Later Mrs A. Roark (married 1939).
Born 6 October 1905, Berkeley, California, USA.
Singles 1927, 1928, 1929, 1930, 1932, 1933, 1935, 1938.
Doubles 1924, 1927, 1930.
Mixed 1929.
Other successes:
US Championships, singles 1923, 1924, 1925, 1927, 1928, 1929, 1931; doubles 1922, 1924, 1925, 1928; mixed 1924, 1928.
French Championships, singles 1928, 1929, 1930, 1932; doubles 1930, 1932.
Olympic gold medals (2) 1924.
Member US Wightman Cup team 1923-38; captain 1930, 1932.

MORTIMER, Florence Angela Margaret
Later Mrs J.E. Barrett (married 1967).
Born 21 April 1932, Plymouth, Devon, England.
Singles 1961.
Doubles 1955.
Other successes:
French Championships, singles 1955.
Australian Championships, singles 1958.
Member British Wightman Cup team 1953-61; captain 1964-70.

NAVRATILOVA, Martina
Born 18 October 1956, Prague, Czechoslovakia.
Singles 1978, 1979, 1982, 1983.
Doubles 1976, 1979, 1981, 1982, 1983.

Other successes:
US Championships, singles 1983; doubles 1977, 1980, 1983.
French Championships singles, 1982; doubles 1975, 1982; mixed 1974.
Australian Championships, singles 1981, 1983; doubles 1975, 1982, 1983.
Italian Championships, doubles 1975.
Member US Wightman Cup team 1983.
Member Czech Federation Cup team 1975; US Federation Cup team 1982.
Granted refugee status in USA in 1975. A left hander.

OSBORNE, Margaret Evelyn, *see* **DU PONT, Mrs W.**

RICE, Helena Bertha Grace (Lena)
Born 21 June 1866, Newinn, Co Tipperary, Ireland.
Died 21 June 1907, Newinn, Co Tipperary, Ireland.
Singles 1890.
Other success:
Irish Championships, mixed 1889.

ROBB, Muriel Evelyn
Born 13 May 1878, Newcastle upon Tyne, Northumberland, England.
Died 12 February 1907, Newcastle upon Tyne, Northumberland, England.
Singles 1902.
Other successes:
Wimbledon non-championship doubles 1902; mixed 1900.
Irish Championships, singles 1901.
Scottish Championships, singles 1901.
Welsh Championships, singles 1899.

ROUND, Dorothy Edith
Later Mrs D.L. Little (married 1937).
Born 13 July 1909, Dudley, Worcestershire, England.
Singles 1934, 1937.
Mixed 1934, 1935, 1936.
Other successes:
Australian Championships, singles 1935.
Member British Wightman Cup team 1931-6.

SMITH, Margaret, *see* **COURT, Mrs Barry M.**

STERRY, Mrs A.
Formerly Charlotte Cooper (married 1901).
Born 22 September 1870, Ealing, Middlesex, England.
Died 10 October 1966, Helensburgh, Scotland.

Singles 1895, 1896, 1898, 1901, 1908.
Other successes:
Wimbledon non-championship doubles 1901, 1902;
  mixed 1901, 1902.
Olympic gold medals (2) 1900.
Irish Championships, singles 1895, 1898; mixed 1895,
  1896, 1899, 1900.
Scottish Championships, singles 1899.
Played hockey for Surrey.

SUSMAN, Mrs J.R.
Formerly Karen J. Hantze (married 1961).
Born 11 December 1942, San Diego, California, U S A.
Singles 1962.
Doubles 1961, 1962.
Other successes:
U S Championships, doubles 1964.
Member U S Wightman Cup team 1960-2, 1965;
  Federation Cup team 1964.

SUTTON, May Godfray
Later Mrs T.C. Bundy (married 1912).
Born 25 September 1886, Plymouth, Devon, England.
Died 4 October 1975, Santa Monica, California, U S A.
Singles 1905, 1907.
Other successes:
U S Championships, singles 1904; doubles 1904.
Wimbledon non-championship doubles 1906; mixed
  1907.
Welsh Championships, singles 1905.

Member U S Wightman Cup team 1925.
She played as an American and was the first overseas
  challenger to become a Wimbledon champion.

WADE, Sarah Virginia
Born 10 July 1945, Bournemouth, England.
Singles 1977.
Other successes:
U S Championships, singles 1968; doubles 1973, 1975.
French Championships, doubles 1973.
Australian Championships, singles 1972; doubles
  1973.
Italian Championships, singles 1971; doubles 1968,
  1971, 1973.
Member British Wightman Cup team 1965-83.
Member British Federation Cup team 1967-83.
Member of All England Club Management
  Committee.

WATSON, Maud Edith Eleanor, MBE
Born 9 October 1864, Harrow, Middlesex, England.
Died 5 June 1946, Charmouth, Dorset, England.
Singles 1884, 1885.
Other successes:
Irish Championships, singles 1884, 1885; mixed 1884,
  1885.
Welsh Championships, singles 1887.

WILLS, Helen N., *see* MOODY, Mrs F.S.

Index

Page numbers in italic refer to illustrations

Aitchison, Mrs H. *34*
Alexandra, Queen *32*
Ali, Muhammad 44
All England Lawn Tennis and
  Croquet Club 14, 21, 129
Alvarez, Lilli de *57*, 59, 106
American Lawn Tennis 101
Aussem, Cilli *57*, *58*
Austin, Henry Wilfred 76
Austin, Tracy 157, 160, *166*
Australian Championships 87,
  111, 113, 117, 155

Baker Fleitz, Beverly 94, *96*, 149
Barker, Sue 137
Barkowitz, Peaches 153
Bath tournament 14, 17
Beasley, E. 13
Bellamy, Rex 135, 139
Betz, Pauline 77, *77*, *78*, *79*, 80,
  80, 81, 82, 83, 85, *85*, 86, 133,
  162

Beverly Hills Tennis Club 82
Bingley, Blanche (later Blanche
  Hillyard) 19, 21, 22, *22*, 31,
  34, 46
Boothby, Dora *32*, *34*, *47*
Borg, Bjorn 24, 51, 131
Borotra, Jean 48, 50
Bostock, Jean 79
Brinker, Norman 96, *96*
Brisbane, Arthur 71
Brookes, Norman 82, 113
Brough, Louise 67, 77, *77*, *79*,
  81, *82*, 83, 84, 85, 86, 87, 91,
  93, *95*, *96*, 103
Budge, Don 82
Bueno, Maria 14, 37, 87, 105,
  105, 106, *106*, 107, *107*, 108,
  108, 109, *110*, 111, *111*, 112,
  112, 114, *116*, 118, 121, 123,
  123, 126, 128, 129, 142, 154
Bullitt, Mrs *see* Stammers, Kay
Bundy, Dodo *77*

Burrows, F.R. 22, 29, 48, *58*
Buxton, Angela *96*

Cannes tournament *42*, 44
Carlton Club, Cannes 44, *44*
Casals, Rosie, *130*, 139, *142*, 156
Cawley, Evonne *see* Goolagong
  Cawley, Evonne
Cawley, Kelly 156
Cheltenham tournament 14
Church Road (later Wimbledon
  site) 43
Cleather, Norah Gordon 29, 55,
  58, 80
Connolly, Cindy and Brenda 92
Connolly, Maureen 70, 83, 86,
  87, *87*, *88*, 89, *89*, 90, 91, *91*,
  92, *92*, 93, *93*, 94, *94*, 95, *95*,
  96, *96*, 106, 158, 162
Connors, Jimmy 133, 176
Palfrey Cooke, Sarah 47, 81
Cooper, Ashley 113

Cooper, Charlotte *see* Sterry,
  Charlotte
Court, Barry 118
Court, Danny 120, 156
Court, Margaret (née Smith) 36,
  67, 87, 94, 107, 108, 109, *109*,
  112, 113, *113*, 114, *114*, *115*,
  116, 117, *117*, 118, *118*, 119,
  119, 120, *120*, 121, 123, *124*,
  125, 126, 128, 132, 133, 134,
  135, *135*, 141, 151, *152*, 153,
  154, 155, 156, 157, 160, 162,
  168, 170, 172
Crawford, Jack 113

Davis Cup 95, 119, 170
Diana, Princess of Wales *176*
Dietrich, Marlene 71
Dod, Ann *17*, 19
Dod, Lottie 17, *17*, 18, *18*, 19,
  19, 21, 22, 23, 24, *47*

Doherty, Reginald Frank and Hugh Lawrence 76
Drobny, Jaroslav *95*
Du Pont, Margaret *see* Osborne Du Pont, Margaret
Du Pont, William 85
Duran, Roberto 63
Durie, Jo 19, *168*
Durr, Françoise 131, 139

Eaton, Hubert 101
Edgbaston tournament 14
Edgington, Mrs 34
Edwards, Vic 152
Eisel, Mary Ann 131
Elizabeth I I, Queen *102*, *146*, 148
Emerson, Roy 141
English Hard Court Championships 129
Evert, Colette *158*
Evert, Jeannie *158*
Evert-Lloyd, Chris 17, 29 51, *119*, *128*, 129, 131, 148, 151, 153, *154*, 155, 156, 157, *157*, 158, *158*, 160, *160*, 161, 162, *163*, 164, 165, *165*, 166, *167*, 168, *168-9*, 170, *170*, *173*, 176, 177, 179, *179*
Exmouth tournament 14, *18*

Fageros, Karol *103*, 104
Flushing Meadow 105
Foreman, George 44
Forest Hills 77, 91, 101
Fraser, Neale 85, 113
French Open Championships 69, 87, 92, 104, 111, 113, 117, 134, 136, 155, 157, 179
Fry, Shirley 92, 93, 94, *96*, 103
Fuller, William 'Pop' 57

Gibson, Althea 94, 97, *97*, 98, *98*, 99, *99*, *100*, 101, *101*, *102*, 103, *103*, *104*, 104, 105
Godfree, Kitty (née McKane) 42, *47*, 55, 57, *57*
Goolagong Cawley, Evonne 24, 37, 75, 126, 129, 130, *130*, 131, *142*, *143*, 149, *149*, *150*, 151, *151*, *152*, 153, *153*, 154, *154*, 155, *155*, 156, *156*, 164, 170, 172, 176

Haas, Robert 177
Hannam, Mrs 34
Hard, Darlene *102*, 104, 111, *121*, 123
Hardy, Bert 99
Harrison, James R. 60
Hart, Doris 77, *77*, 79, 83, 84–5, *86*, 92, 96
Heldman, Gladys 129
Henrotin, Sylvia 69
Hillyard, Commander George 19, 21, 24, 29, 30, 31
Hillyard, Mrs *see* Bingley, Blanche
Hoad, Lew 113
Holman, Mrs *34*

Hopman, Harry 95, 119
Hopman, Nell 95, 96, 119
Horvath, Kathy 179
Hunt, Lesley 131

International Lawn Tennis Federation 129
Irish Championships 14
Italian Championships 113

Jacobs, Helen 43, 51, 57, *59*, 63, 64, *64*, 68, *70*, 83, 179
Jaeger, Andrea 134, 160, *163*, 181
Janes, Christine *see* Truman, Christine
Johnson, Robert 101
Jones, Ann 112, *112*, 117, 129, 135, 138, 139, *140*, 141, *141*
Jones, C.M. 63, 73, 95, 111
Jordan, Kathy 157, 170

Kennedy, John F. 124
Kent, Duchess of *176*
King, Billy Jean (née Moffitt) 24, 36, 67, 75, 76, 97, 98, 104, 109, 111, 112, 113, 114, *116*, 117, 118, 119, 120, 121, *121*, *122*, 123, *123*, 124, *124*, *125*, 126, *126*, *127*, 128, *128*, 129, *130*, 131, *131*, 132, *132*, 133, *133*, 134, *134*, 138, 139, 141, *141*, *142*, 147, 149, 153, 156, 157, *157*, *159*, 160, 162, 164, 168, 170, *173*, 177
Krahwinkel, Hilde *see* Sperling, Hilde
Kramer, Jack 133

Lacoste, Jean René 76
Lambert Chambers, Dorothea 25, *25*, 27, 29, 30, 31, *32*, 33, *33*, *34*, 36, *36*, 37, *37*, 38, *47*, 134, 162
Larcombe, Ethel *34*, *35*, 36, 38, *47*
Laver, Rod, 113, 129, 131, 141
Lawford, Herbert *12*
Lawn Tennis Association 129
Lawn Tennis for Ladies 25
Lendl, Ivan 174
Lenglen, Charles 35, 36, 38, 47
Lenglen, Suzanne 17, 35, *35*, 36, *36*, 37, *37*, 38, *38*, *39*, *40*, *41*, 42, *42*, 43, *43*, 44, 44, 45, *45*, *46*, 47, *47*, 48, *48*, *49*, 50, *50*, 57, *61*, 84, 87, 89, 133, 134, 151, 162, 182
Leonard, Sugar Ray 63
Lieberman, Nancy 177
Lloyd, John 170
Lombard, Carole 71

McCall, George 139
MacDonald, Jeanette 71
McEnroe, John 38, 60
McGeehan, W.O. 60
McKane, Kitty *see* Godfree, Kitty
McNair, Mrs *34*
Mallory, Molla 42, *42*

Mandlikova, Hana *164*, 165, 174
Marble, Alice 50, 63, 67, 68, *68*, 69, *69*, 70, *70*, 71, *71*, *72*, 73, *73*, *74*, 75, *75*, 76, *76*, 79, 81, 91, 93, 95, *97*, 101, 132, 172
Marble, Dan 68
Marina, Princess of Kent *86*, *91*
Mary, Queen *46*, 48, *78*
Maskell, Dan 72
Mayer, Gene 149
Moody, Freddie 66
Moran, Gussy 83, *84*, *85*
Morozova, Olga *130*
Mortimer, Angela 104, 107, 109, 111, 135, 136, *136*, 137, 138, *138*, *139*, 141
Morton, Miss 30–1
Mountbatten, Lord Louis and Lady Edwina *78*

Navratilova, Martina 67, 94–5, 111, 112, 134, 155, 164, 165, 166, 168, 170, 171, *171*, 172, *172*, *173*, 174, *174*, *175*, 176, 177, *177*, 178, 179, *179*, *180*, *181*, 182, *182*
Newcombe, John 119–20
Nichols, Stan 118
Nicklaus, Jack 123
Northern Tournament (Manchester) 17

Olliff, John 52, 73, 74, 82
O'Neill, Mrs *34*
Osborne Du Pont, Margaret 67, 77, *77*, 81, 83, *83*, 84, 85, *121*

Pacific Southwest Open Championships 127
Parton, Mrs *34*
Partridge, Susan 93
Patterson, Gerald 113
Payot, Mlle *58*

Queens Tennis Club 33, 84, 89

Renshaw, Ernest *12*, *18*, 22
Renshaw, William *12*, 14, 23
Reynolds, Sandra 111
Richards, Renée 177, 179
Richey, Nancy *121*
Riggs, Bobby *74*, 75–6, 82, 132, 133–4, *133*
Robb, Muriel 23
Roberts, Arthur 137
Rogers, Ginger 103
Rose, Mervyn 124, 126
Rosewall, Ken 113, 119, 120
Round, Dorothy 57, *59*, 59
Ryan, Elizabeth 17, 35, *38*, *39*, 42, 44, 59, *61*, *173*

Satterthwaite, Mrs *34*
Seal, Bea 84, 94, 138, 148
Sedgeman, Frank 113, 118
Shaw, George Bernard 51, 66
Smith, Margaret *see* Court, Margaret
Smith, Stan 133
Sperling, Hilde (née Krahwinkel) 57, *59*, 67, *67*

Stammers, Kay (later Mrs Bullitt) 71, *72*, *73*, 73, 79, 82, 85, 172
Sterry, Charlotte (née Cooper), 29, 30, *30*, 34, 47
Stolle, Fred 141
Susman, Karen (née Hautze) *109*, 111, *121*, 126
Sutton, May (later Bundy) 28, 29, 30–1, 33, 77
Swanson, Gloria 74

Taylor, Roger 131
Teeguarden, Jerry 147
Tegart, Judy 129
Tennant, Eleanor 'Teach' 70, 71, 75, 81, *87*, 89, 91, 92, 93, 95, 111
Tilden, Big Bill 43, 133, 156
Tingay, Lance 57, 77, 92, 94, 96, 105
Tinling, Teddy 84, 99, 106, 112, 133, 141, *142*
Todd, Pat 77
Truman, Christine (later Mrs Janes) 106, *135*, 136, 137, *137*, 138, *139*, 141, 174
Tuckey, Mrs *34*
Tulloch, Mrs *34*
Twynam, Mrs 154

U S Championships 42, 44, 51–2, 68, 73, 76, 77, 79, 81, 84, 87, 89, 91, 92, 93, 96, 97, 101, 104, 105, 111, 113, 117, 120, 126, 131, 134, 148, 149, 155, 157, 179
U S Lawn Tennis Association 129

Varner, Margaret *121*
Virginia Slims tour 119, 129, 131, 157

Wade, Virginia 29, 87, 107, 135, 136, 138, 141, 142, *142*, *143*, *144*, *146*, 147, *147*, 148, *148*, 154, *159*, 170
Wagner, Robert F. *104*
Ward, Pat 103
Watson, Lilian 11, *12*, *13*, 17
Watson, Maud *12*, 13, *13*, 14, 17, 21, *47*, 182
Wightman, Mrs Hazel 42, 112, 133
Wightman Cup 63, 68, 71, 77, 79, *121*, 138
Wilberforce, Sir Herbert 57
Wills Moody, Helen 17, 43, 44, 45, *45*, 47, 48, 51, *51*, *52*, 52, *53*, *54*, 55, *55*, 56, 57, *57*, 58, *58*, 59, 60, *60*, *61*, 62, 63, 64, *64*, 65, 66, *66*, 67, 68, 73, 84, 91–2, 95, 112, 155, 162
Wilson, Connie 31
Wingfield, Major Walter Clapton 14
Women's Tennis Association 131, 170
World Tennis 129
Worple Road (original Wimbledon site) 14, *20*, 43

Acknowledgements

A great many people have been extremely helpful in the preparation of this book, and the publisher, on behalf of Miss Wade and Miss Rafferty, would particularly like to thank the following for all their assistance: Valerie Warren, Assistant Curator of the Wimbledon Lawn Tennis Museum and the rest of the staff, whose patient and enthusiastic help both with picture research and information from the library was unstinting and essential; Lance Tingay, the well-known tennis writer for permission to reproduce biographical records that originally appeared in his book *100 Years of Wimbledon* (Guinness Superlatives Limited, 1977), and for so kindly agreeing to update the information; C.M. Jones for the loan of his watercolour painting of Miss Suzanne Lenglen; all the champions and players, particularly Bea Seal, who so generously took time to discuss their memories of Wimbledon, especially Mrs Bullitt (Miss Kay Stammers), Miss Helen Jacobs, and Mrs Du Pont (Miss Margaret Osborne) who in addition loaned personal photographs for inclusion in this book.

Photographic Acknowledgements:

The publisher has endeavoured to acknowledge all copyright holders of the pictures reproduced in this book. However, in view of the complexity of securing copyright information, should any photographs not be correctly attributed, then the publisher undertakes to make any appropriate changes in future editions of this book.

Allsport: 180; Arthur Cole & Michael Cole, Le Roye Productions: vi, 35 (right), 42, 74 (left), 76, 77 (top), 86 (above right), 95 (top right), 100, 101, 103, 105, 106 (left), 108 (left), 109, 114, 115, 116 (left and centre right), 117, 118, 123 (left and right), 125 (above and below), 127, 128, 130 (above and below), 132 (left), 133, 135, 136, 138, 139 (above and below), 140, 141 (above and below), 142 (above and below), 143, 144, 145, 146, 147, 149, 150, 151 (above and below), 152 (above and below), 154, 155, 158, 160, 161, 163 (left and right), 164, 165 (left), 167 (left and right), 169, 171, 172-173 (top), 173 (below), 174 (left and right), 175 (left and right), 177, 178, 179, 181 (left), 182; Associated Press: 87; BBC Hulton Picture Library: iii, 26, 27, 29, 32 (top left), 33, 35 (top left), 38 (top), 39, 40-41, 41, 44 (below left), 45, 48, 49, 51, 53, 55 (top far right), 57, 58 (right), 60, 61 (left and top right), 62, 66 (left and right), 67, 68, 69 (above and below), 74 (above), 79 (below right), 80, 81, 88, 91 (above), 96 (top and below left), 98 (top), 99, 106 (right), 107, 116 (above and below), 119, 120, 122, 124, 126, 131, 132 (right), 150 (top left), 153, 156, 157, 159; Express Newspapers: 134; Fox Photos: 83, 89, 90, 91 (below), 92 (left), 94; Freelance Photographers Guild: 52, 84, 97, 98 (below), 102 (top), 104; Helen Jacobs: 59 (below), 64 (top); Kay Stammers: 74 (top); Keystone Press Agency: 75, 77 (below), 79 (below left), 92 (right), 96 (below left); Mansell Collection: 14-15, 18 (below), 19, 20-21, 22-23 (centre), 24, 34 (far left), 46 (left), 54; Margaret Osborne Du Pont: 113, 121; New Yorker: 50; Popperfoto: 85; S & G Picture Agency: 25 (right), 31 (right) 32 (below left), 71, 95 (top left and bottom), 110, 111, 165 (right), 181 (left); Syndication International: 40 (top left), 108 (top right and below), 112; Tommy Hindley: ii, 148, 162 (above and below), 166, 168 (left), 170, 176; Wimbledon Museum: 11, 12, 13, 16, 17, 18 (left), 22 (left), 23 (right), 25 (top), 28, 30-31 (centre), 30 (top left), 36, 37 (left and right), 38 (left), 43, 44 (top), 46-47, 58 (left), 59 (top), 61 (below right), 63 (above and below), 64 (below), 65, 70 (above and below), 74 (below), 75, 78 (top left, right and below), 82, 86 (top left), 93, 102 (below), 137;

Colour plates: between pages 48/49: Glasgow Art Gallery and Museum: first page; Michael Dempsey: second page; Wimbledon Tennis Museum: third page and fourth page (above); C.M. Jones: fourth page (below); between pages 112/113: Arthur Cole & Michael Cole, Le Roye Productions: first page (above and below); second page (left), third page (above and below), fourth page; All Sport: second page (centre); between pages 128/129: Tommy Hindley: first page, third page (below centre), Arthur Cole & Michael Cole, Le Roye Productions: second page, third page (top left), fourth page (right); Wimbledon Tennis Museum: third page (right); S & G: fourth page (top left); between pages 176/177: Arthur Cole & Michael Cole, Le Roye Productions: first page (top right); Tommy Hindley: first page (right), second page (left), third page (above and below), fourth page.